D1591335

CANADIAN PACIFIC

The Golden Age of Travel

BARRY LANE

GOOSE LANE

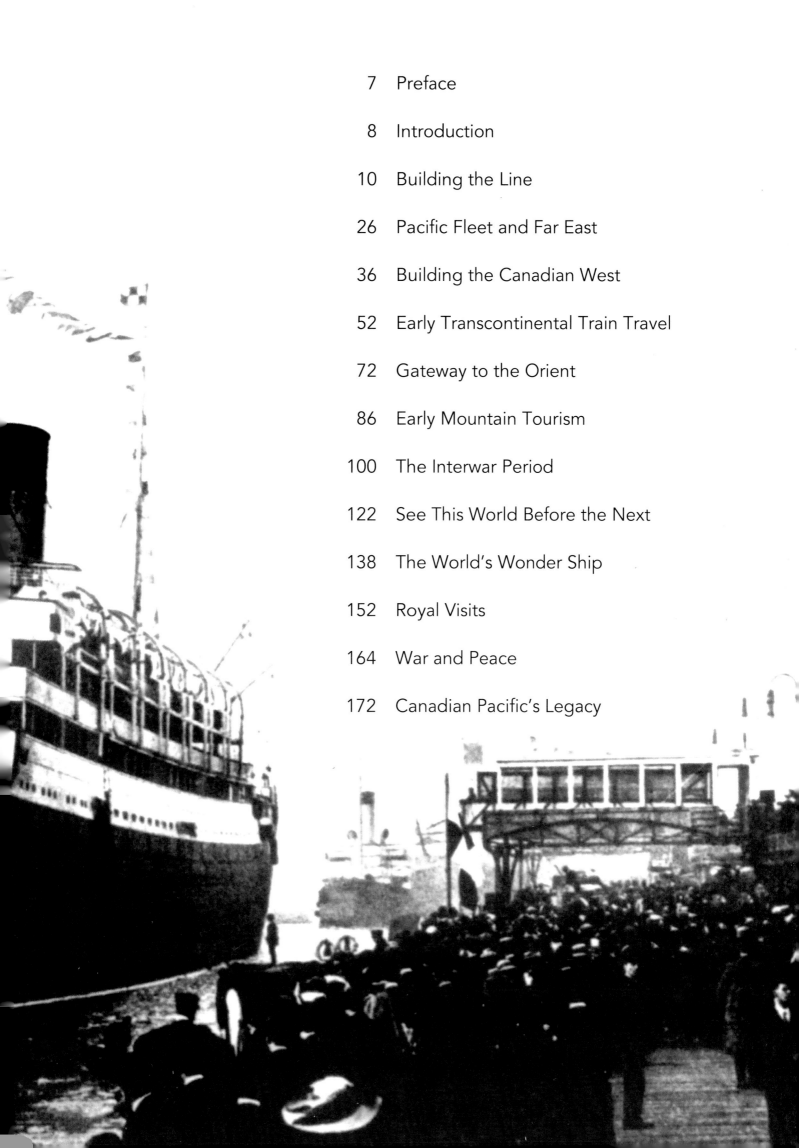

RESORTS IN THE ROCKIES

CANADIAN PACIFIC

Preface

As someone who has had the privilege of accompanying numerous groups travelling by rail across Canada and lecturing to them on the history of Canadian Pacific and its global transportation system, I have long wanted to relate this important story to a wider audience.

Many publications tell different elements of this story —the building of the line, the creation of the fleets, the hotels, and the romance of early rail tourism—but none of them put all these elements together in a visual fashion that makes Canadian Pacific's achievements accessible to a general audience.

Anyone in the field owes a great deal of gratitude to E.J. Hart, former director of the Whyte Museum of the Canadian Rockies and author of the groundbreaking work, *The Selling of Canada: The CPR and the Beginnings of Canadian Tourism*. As well, the works of historians W. Kaye Lamb and Robert Turner and the publications of former Canadian Pacific archivist David Laurence Jones, provide essential reading on the subject.

I would like to thank the numerous archives across Canada that have helped make possible the publication of this work through the online digitalization of their visual collections. Such access has allowed me to use many images that the general public has never seen. A special vote of thanks goes to the archivists of the Chung Collection at the University of British Columbia, the Glenbow Museum in Calgary, and those at the CP Archives in Montreal.

I would also like to mention my associate of thirty years, David Mendel, who inspired me to write this book; publishers Sylvain Harvey and Goose Lane Editions, and art director, André Durocher; Luc Antoine Couturier, an outstanding colleague and photographer; and finally, my brother Bob Lane, of Lane Realty Corporation, Regina, Saskatchewan, whose generosity made this publication possible. Our grandfathers, one from Lincolnshire and the other from Alsace Lorraine, broke the prairie sod in 1900 in what would later become the province of Saskatchewan. The story of their emigration and successful settlement in the Canadian West is a part of this great Canadian Pacific legacy.

BARRY LANE

Facing page: Canadian Pacific brochure cover, 1931. Artist E.A. Odell.

Preceding pages: The *Empress of Ireland* leaving Liverpool, 1909

Frontispiece: An early, east bound, Canadian Pacific transcontinental on the famous "Loops," climbing up into Roger's Pass in the Selkirk Mountains of British Columbia

Introduction

The epic tale of Canadian Pacific's worldwide transportation empire is one of Canada's greatest success stories. The largest and most complete travel system humanity has ever known, the company straddled half the globe for over fifty years, helped build the nation we know as Canada today, and even created the international image and reputation that are still associated with the country. No ordinary enterprise, the history of Canadian Pacific is inextricably linked with the birth and flourishing of the young nation called Canada.

In 1885, Canadian Pacific completed over 3,200 kilometres (2,000 miles) of railway track, linking Montreal to the Pacific Ocean and creating Canada's first transcontinental railway system. The company then established fleets of vessels on the Pacific and Atlantic Oceans, laying the foundation of an imperial dream: the "All Red Line," a transportation route that allowed British citizens to travel around the world, always visiting territories within their Empire, painted red on the maps of the day.

George Stephen, the founder and president of Canadian Pacific, called the line the new route to the Orient, an acknowledgement of the long-sought Northwest Passage. It was this link with the exotic Orient that made Canadian Pacific special. Hong Kong, Shanghai, Nagasaki, and Yokohama were all regular ports of call for Canadian Pacific ships, which carried passengers and brought high-value cargoes of silk, tea, and opium back to North America and Europe.

Canadian Pacific's travel empire was unique. No other transportation system in world history would succeed in running such a complete, interlocking system, with large fleets of first-class vessels operating across two different oceans at the same time, linked by fast continental express trains of the highest quality. The scope of the system was breathtaking.

To enhance the traveller's experience while voyaging across Canada, the company constructed castle-like railway hotels, such as the Chateau Frontenac in Quebec City and the Banff Springs Hotel in the Rocky Mountains, as well as impressive railway stations that reflected the majesty and romance of the land. With their romantic profiles and aristocratic service, the hotels proved so popular with Canadians and foreign visitors that they became veritable symbols and landmarks of the country. Many of the train stations remain in use today and stand as proud reminders of Canadian Pacific's contribution to the building of the nation.

All of this system was an integral part of the legendary beauty and romance of the Golden Age of Travel. Early travellers so enjoyed the route's outstanding scenery, extraordinary engineering feats, and fine service that Canadian Pacific's transcontinental train trip became renowned as one of the world's great railway journeys, along with the contemporary Orient Express and the Trans-Siberian Railway.

Facing page: Early Canadian Pacific travel poster/postcard

Overleaf: Donald Smith drives home the Last Spike for the Canadian Pacific Railway on November 7, 1885. William Van Horne and railway engineer Sandford Fleming stand behind him.

CANADIAN PACIFIC
THE EMPIRE'S GREATEST
RAILWAY

BUILDING THE LINE

The very geography of the place presented a monumental challenge to the building of the Canada we know today. Unlike the United States, which has a fertile Midwest connecting the eastern and western portions of the country, an enormous expanse of wilderness known as the Canadian Shield separates Canada's best agricultural land from the eastern part of the country. The latter represents over 5 million square kilometres (2 million square miles) of rocky outcroppings, endless lakes, and seemingly bottomless muskeg, with its great boreal forest reaching to eternity. In the early days, the only way to cross this wilderness was via canoe along the rivers or lakes, or else one could travel south through the United States to reach the Canadian West. Neither option offered a viable approach for the long-term building of the Canadian nation.

As a result of this situation, as late as 1870, the Canadian West remained virtually empty of any white settlement. The plains were still the domain of Aboriginal buffalo hunters and their Métis (mixed-blood First Nations and white) counterparts, while beyond the mountains lived the indigenous coastal peoples of British Columbia. Up until this time, much of the region was known as Rupert's Land and was under the control of the Hudson's Bay Company, the great fur trading monopoly. By 1869, however, the directors of the HBC had decided to sell most of their lands to the new country of Canada, founded in 1867.

The question of control over what would become the Canadian West was of great concern to the government of the day. As early as the 1840s, thousands of American settlers headed west along the Oregon Trail, their presence representing a potential threat to the ownership of the empty lands further north. Combined with this challenge was the popular concept of American manifest destiny, which hoped to see the Stars and Stripes flying over as much of the North American continent as possible.

The pressures of American expansionism were felt especially among the fledgling colonies of Vancouver Island and British Columbia. In 1866, they joined together and in 1871 British Columbia became part of the Dominion of Canada with the stipulation that within ten years the government of Canada would complete a transcontinental railway to join the west coast to the rest of the country.

The building of this railway, however, was easier said than done. To meet the demands of British Columbia, within those ten years almost 4,800 kilometres (3,000 miles) of railway track would need to be laid through some of the most rugged terrain in the world. The line would have to be built not only through the Rocky Mountains and the difficult interior of British Columbia but also across the 1,600-kilometre (1,000-mile) width of the Canadian Shield, a wilderness many non-indigenous people believed impenetrable.

A comparison with the building of the first continental line in the United States gives a sense of the challenge facing the young dominion. The US line was 2,856 kilometres (1,775 miles) in length and started as far west as the Missouri River in Nebraska. It took six years to build and was only completed, with the greatest difficulty, in 1869. At the time, the population of the United States was close to forty million; in contrast, Canada's population during the construction of its first transcontinental was approximately four million. If the American experience served as an example, the building of such a railway across Canada would be a daunting task indeed.

The challenges involved in the building of the railway, and the resulting political turmoil, meant that only 1,448 kilometres (900 miles) of track had been completed by

Facing page: The wife of a Hudson's Bay Company official, Frances Hopkins, accompanied her husband through the Canadian wilderness and painted her experiences. She sits with her husband in a giant "canoe de maître" as its French-Canadian "voyageur" crew "shoots" the Lachine Rapids above Montreal, June 1863.

Below: Blackfoot warriors of the Brave Dog Warrior Society, c. 1913. Located in what is now southern Alberta and northern Montana, the Blackfoot Nation was among the most powerful of the confederations of native peoples on the northern plains.

1881. Under pressure from British Columbia to finish the line, the government decided to turn the task over to a private consortium called the Canadian Pacific Railway and gave it another ten years to complete the job. The president of the consortium was a Scotsman, George Stephen, who had arrived almost penniless in Canada in 1844. By sheer brilliance and financial wizardry, he rose rapidly in Montreal society to become one of Canada's most successful businessmen and the head of the Bank of Montreal.

Stephen used his abilities and political connections to negotiate with the Canadian government one of the most extraordinary deals in North American railway history. First and foremost, he got twenty-five million acres of land "fairly fit for settlement," which meant that Canadian Pacific could pick the best land in the Canadian West for its land grants, in some cases going as much as a hundred miles away from the main line to make its choices. In contrast, the American transcontinentals in most cases received alternating sections, both good land and bad, within ten miles of their track. What was common to both countries, though,

was their treatment of the indigenous peoples, who were deliberately pushed aside to allow the construction of the railways across their ancestral lands.

The second exceptional aspect of the deal was that Canadian Pacific received $25 million to build the line, an amount which would ultimately rise to almost $75 million when all the subsidies and equipment were included, an inordinate sum for the time, particularly considering the small population base.

Finally, and most important of all, the consortium received a virtual monopoly over all railway traffic in the West for the next twenty years. This meant the Canadian West would become Canadian Pacific's fiefdom, making the company one of the richest and most powerful in the world.

In late 1881, after a slow first year of construction, George Stephen decided to hire William Van Horne as general manager. An American of Dutch descent and only thirty-nine at the time of his arrival in Canada, Van Horne was well known in the American Midwest as a prodigy able to resuscitate insolvent railways.

One of Canadian history's most colourful figures, this railway builder was a Renaissance man with an extraordinary range of capabilities, vast general knowledge on a multitude of subjects, and an unrelenting love for life. In the face of enormous difficulties, his abilities and leadership led to the rapid completion of the CPR in 1885, five years in advance of the government's deadline.

In 1884, Van Horne was appointed vice-president of the line; he replaced George Stephen as president in 1888. Working in this capacity until his retirement in 1899, Van Horne laid the groundwork for the expansion of the CPR as a successfully integrated transportation and communication system, with telegraph services and freight delivery, luxury hotels along the line, and a fleet of first-class vessels on the Pacific Ocean. In 1900, his work completed in Canada, he turned his energies south to Cuba, reorganizing its railway system with the construction of a trunk line across the island and the development of numerous related industries. In recognition of his achievements, he was knighted by Queen Victoria in 1894. When he died on September 11, 1915, at the age of seventy-two, Canadian Pacific ceased its operations around the world for twenty-four hours as a token of its esteem for William Van Horne.

Canadian Pacific constructed its 3,200-kilometre (2,000-mile) part of the line in segments, with crews working simultaneously across the Canadian Shield, the Canadian prairies, and the mountain chains and river canyons of Alberta and British Columbia; the first transcontinental railway in the United States and the Russian Trans-Siberian also used this approach. Many historians regard the line, constructed across some of the world's roughest terrain, as one of the great engineering feats of the nineteenth century.

On November 7, 1885, in central British Columbia, Donald Smith (later Lord Strathcona) drove home the Last Spike at Craigellachie, a site named for the rallying cry of the Grant Clan in Banffshire, northern Scotland. Both Smith and his cousin George Stephen, the two major forces behind the construction of the line, had grown up close by this historic Scottish landmark. Sandford Fleming, an outstanding engineer who played a key part in the development of the line and was one of the first promoters of standard time, was also of Scottish origin. Although at this time the Scots in Canada made up only 15 percent of the total English-speaking population, they provided over 50 percent of the leadership of the country, excelling in politics, business, and education. As in many other British settler colonies, the Scots were the true foot soldiers of empire.

William Van Horne was also present for the driving of the Last Spike. A gruff man who did not like pomp and ceremony, his only words to the crowd that day were, "The line has been built well in every way."

Top: George Stephen, the founder and first president of the Canadian Pacific Railway. This famous portrait was taken in the Montreal studios of the Notman brothers in 1871.

Bottom: William Van Horne. The leader and long-time president of the Canadian Pacific Railway. Notman studios, 1886.

Facing page: The Great Bluff at 88 Mile Post on the Thompson River, British Columbia, c. 1867. BC's mountainous topography obliged Canadian Pacific to construct its line along the canyon walls of both the Fraser and Thompson Rivers, where wagon roads were built in the early 1860s gold rush.

The Northwest Rebellion

In spite of the line's rapid progress under William Van Horne, Canadian Pacific faced severe financial problems and came very close to bankruptcy in the spring of 1885. In early April of that year, starving Cree, an indigenous tribe in the District of Saskatchewan, accused the Canadian government of failing to meet the terms of its treaties with them and mounted a rebellion. At the same time, the Métis, concerned that unnegotiated government surveys of their settlements posed a threat to their ownership of their land, launched a rebellion under the leadership of Louis Riel. The Canadian Pacific transported troops on its still-incomplete railway to the district of Saskatchewan to quell the rebellions, and in gratitude the Canadian government granted a further loan that allowed the CPR to avoid insolvency and complete the construction of its line. It is profoundly ironic that the Northwest Rebellion against the very changes the railway was bringing to the Western territories was the key element that led to the transcontinental's successful completion.

Above: Troops on board the Canadian Pacific railway on their way to the Northwest Rebellion in early April 1885.

THE SOUTHERN ROUTE THROUGH THE MOUNTAINS

Originally, Canadian Pacific planned a route through the Yellowhead Pass, which offered the company a relatively easy passage through the eastern mountains of British Columbia. At the very last moment, however, in 1881, the company decided to shift the railway far to the south. This decision allowed Canadian Pacific to shorten the line by over 320 kilometres (200 miles), which reduced initial construction costs and, more importantly, allowed CP to cut off future American competition from the south. The line travelled across the southern prairies, through the Kicking Horse Pass in the Rocky Mountains and Rogers Pass in the Selkirk Mountains of the Columbia Range. The trajectory involved an incredible gamble, as it was unknown at the time if a feasible path even existed through the Selkirks.

This new southern route forced the railway to lay its track along the sides of towering mountains, while following the banks of narrow, swiftly flowing mountain streams. The results were often roadbeds with extraordinarily steep grades that presented a threat of flooding and avalanches of rock or snow. Running a railway under such conditions, especially during Canada's severe winter months, would prove very demanding.

To overcome these challenges, Canadian Pacific worked hard to upgrade its route through the mountains by diminishing the grades of the original track. Hundreds of millions of dollars were spent on different projects, and the work still continues today. For the tourist, this decision to move the line to the south brought a wonderful visual dividend. With the route's extraordinary scenery and its railroad engineering wizardry of tunnels and bridges, Canadian Pacific's western route became renowned among the travelling public.

———

Below: A 1923 map showing the principal lines of the CPR

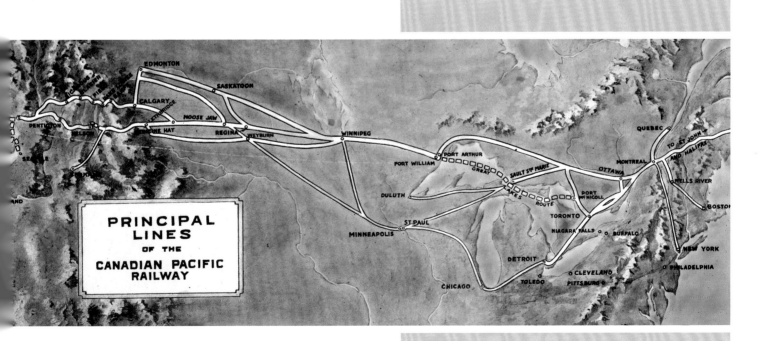

PRINCIPAL
LINES
OF THE
CANADIAN PACIFIC
RAILWAY

THE BIG HILL AND THE SPIRAL TUNNELS

The Kicking Horse Pass crosses the Continental Divide at 1,627 metres (5,339 feet) in elevation, the highest point on the Canadian Pacific line. The track then drops down the spectacular valley of the Kicking Horse River. Initially, the rushing waters of the river run far below the line, while the mountains rise directly above. Towering over the valley is the extraordinary Mount Stephen, named for the president and founder of the line, George Stephen. The mountain offers the most fitting monument possible for the achievements of this self-made man, in later life a close friend of Queen Victoria and the first colonial to be admitted as a member of the House of Lords.

Known as the Big Hill, the pass was always a major bottleneck for the efficiency of the railway. Dropping down more than 300 metres (1,000 feet) over a distance of 16 kilometres (10 miles), the initial railway grade of 4.5 feet per mile made the Big Hill one of the steepest grades on any main-line railway in the world. Initially numerous "pusher engines" were required to help eastern-bound trains climb the heights of the pass. In reverse, descending western-bound trains had to be wary of losing control on the steep descent, and three run-off tracks were constructed to divert runaway trains onto rising slopes to slow them down. Nevertheless, over the next twenty-five years,

numerous freight trains derailed in the pass (the company's passenger trains were more carefully looked after), and the overall efficiency and speed of the line were greatly diminished.

In 1909, Canadian Pacific completed two spiral tunnels, constructed through the interior of the mountains on each side of the pass, to address these problems. Joined together, they form an elongated figure eight, which runs at an angle across the pass and the Kicking Horse River. The tunnels double the length of the climb through the Kicking Horse, allowing the railway a 39-metre (126-foot) change in elevation that brings the grade of the pass down to an acceptable 2.2 feet per mile.

Although this type of railway tunnel was used in Switzerland, these were the only ones ever built for a North American railway. When very long trains travel through the pass, one can actually see the front cars of the train coming out of one of the tunnels while the rear of the train is still entering.

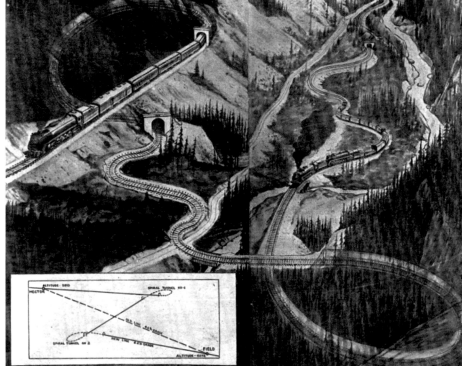

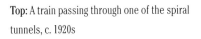

Top: A train passing through one of the spiral tunnels, c. 1920s

Centre: A sketch showing an eastbound train climbing through the Kicking Horse Pass via Canadian Pacific's spiral tunnels

Bottom: The Kicking Horse Pass with Mount Stephen in the centre

Facing page: A train climbing the Big Hill in the Kicking Horse Pass with the aid of four locomotives, c. 1900

THE TRESTLE BRIDGES

By 1884, Canadian Pacific had reached the Rocky Mountains and was already encountering serious financial problems with the continued building of the line. To speed construction through the mountains, the company built dozens of temporary wood trestle bridges, some of them rising almost 90 metres (300 feet) into the air. No other railway in North America built as many high timber bridges as Canadian Pacific did in the western mountains. These spectacular structures were perhaps the greatest testimony to the genius and ability of those who undertook the task of constructing a railway through such terrain.

The challenge was especially acute in the steep Beaver River Valley of the Selkirk Mountains. Here, enormous ravines had to be bridged to bring the line up the side of the valley to reach the eastern approach to Rogers Pass. The bridge constructed over one of these ravines, Mountain Creek, was 50 metres (164 feet) in height and 330 metres (1,086 feet) long. It contained over two million board feet of timber and was claimed to be the largest wooden structure in the world at the time.

However, the most famous of the Beaver Valley bridges was Stoney Creek bridge, which rose 89 metres (292 feet), making it, as the railway claimed, the highest timber railway bridge in the world. In 1893, it was replaced by a metal structure, which was later reinforced by a second set of arches in 1929. It is still in use today, and its crossing is one of the major highlights of any trip along the line.

Right: A work train on Mountain Creek bridge in Beaver Valley, the Selkirk Mountains, 1885

Left: The second Stoney Creek bridge, c. 1920s

Below: The old Ottertail Creek bridge west of Field, British Columbia, in the valley of the Kicking Horse River, 1885

Facing page: Canadian Pacific's "New Highway to the Orient." Crossing the second Stoney Creek bridge in the Selkirk Mountains, c. 1890s

THE CANADIAN PACIFIC

Stony Creek Bridge, Selkirk Mountains.

THE NEW HIGHWAY TO THE ORIENT

ACROSS THE Mountains, Prairies and Rivers of Canada.

ROGERS PASS AND THE LOOPS

After climbing the Beaver Valley to an elevation of 1,330 metres (4,360 feet), the railway entered a narrow valley called Rogers Pass. Major Albert Bowman Rogers, a surveyor, discovered the pass in July 1882, well after the decision had been made to move the main line south and cut through the Selkirk Mountains. Due to the steepness of the terrain, a series of spectacular trestle bridges were constructed to lower the grade on the western side of the pass.

Today, two railway tunnels replace travel through Rogers Pass, both of which pass through Mount Macdonald, located on the southeastern side of the pass. Running one above the other, the upper tunnel, the 8-kilometre (5-mile) Connaught tunnel was completed in 1916, and the lower tunnel, the 14.7-kilometre (9.1-mile) Mount Macdonald tunnel, in 1988. The latter is the longest railway tunnel in the western hemisphere.

The line crossed through the Rockies and the Columbia Mountains (the Purcells, Selkirks, and Monashees) to dramatically different landscape in the semi-desert areas of central British Columbia. There, the line hung breathtakingly along the arid canyon walls of the Thompson River before meeting the mighty Fraser River and another series of stunning canyons running down the divide between the Cascade and Coastal mountain ranges. Finally, the tracks emerged suddenly from the mountains to reach the lush delta area where the Fraser River meets the Pacific Ocean at Vancouver, chosen in 1886 as the railway's western terminus.

CHINESE LABOURERS

Fifteen thousand Chinese labourers brought in for the task from California and southeastern China built, for the most part, the Fraser and Thompson River sections of the line. As was typical of the times, the Chinese were used as cheap labour, paid about half the wages of similar white workers while obliged to undertake the most difficult and dangerous work. They also had to assume additional expenses that their white counterparts did not incur and were often housed in tents that provided little protection from the inclement weather. Malnutrition meant that scurvy became a major problem.

As a result of the poor living conditions and dangerous work, over six hundred Chinese died during the construction of their segment of the line, approximately four men for every mile of track. In 2006, the Canadian government officially apologized to the Chinese-Canadian community for the loss of life and continuing discrimination against Chinese workers that followed the completion of the line.

Top: A 1920s view of a passenger train entering the eastern portal of the Connaught tunnel. Notice that none of the passengers are sitting in the open-air mountain observation car.

Bottom: Chinese workers on the line, 1888–89

Facing page: "The Jaws of Death," the Thompson River Canyon, 1889

PACIFIC FLEET
AND
FAR EAST

The completion of the Canadian transcontinental railway line was a huge achievement. But William Van Horne and George Stephen's ambitious plans for the new company were only beginning. They immediately moved to construct fleets of steamers on the Pacific and Atlantic to help stimulate railway traffic in Canada. Although the company only started its operations on the Atlantic in 1903, these two fleets ultimately made Canadian Pacific unique. No other North American transcontinental railway line directly owned and operated fleets of such scope and scale, for such a long duration, on both the Atlantic and Pacific Oceans. These ships, combined with the railway, gave Canadian Pacific both enormous power and the ability to take its passengers halfway around the world.

The American railway companies had great difficulty in matching Canadian Pacific's monopoly. Serving a much larger population, ownership of their lines was mostly divided into three basic segments: the powerful eastern trunk lines, the Midwest "Granger Lines," and the western transcontinentals, which initially started far to the west, over the Missouri River. The competitive nature of the American system basically ensured that none of these lines would be able to offer the same degree of integrated service that

Canadian Pacific, a single owner, could provide over a long distance to its travellers.

Ultimately, the only American transcontinental to be linked simultaneously by its own shipping lines to both the Atlantic and the Pacific was the Southern Pacific Railway. On the Atlantic, from 1883 to 1942, its vessels provided a freight and passenger service from the line's eastern terminus in New Orleans, to New York City, Havana, and Mexico. However, no transatlantic service was offered by the company, and its vessels were substantially smaller and fewer in number than those of Canadian Pacific's eastern fleet. On the Pacific Ocean, Southern Pacific initiated its own shipping operations in 1874 and continued them until 1915.

THE ALL RED LINE: THE STUFF OF LEGEND

George Stephen called his transportation system "the new route to the Orient," but others called it the "All Red Line" or "All British Empire Route," by which a first-class Englishman could leave Liverpool on a Canadian Pacific ship travelling to Canada, cross the country on CP rail,

Right Hong Kong in 1907.
Taken from Victoria Peak,
Hong Kong Island.

Facing page: *Empress of India*,
first docking in Vancouver, April 28, 1891

Preceding pages: *Empress of Japan*, c. 1891

and then navigate the Pacific on another Canadian Pacific vessel to Hong Kong or Sydney, and never leave the British Empire. It was the stuff of legend.

On April 28, 1891, the first of Canadian Pacific's passenger liners, the *Empress of India*, docked at its home port of Vancouver, completing the company's first round-the-world journey by train and ship. Van Horne himself greeted the ship and the 131 first-class passengers on board, many of whom had participated in the entire journey around the world. The *Empress of India* was soon followed by its sister ships, the *Empress of Japan* and the *Empress of China*. The three vessels offered during the summer sailing season a departure every twenty-one days to the Orient. With an average twelve-and-a-half-day run to Yokohama, the ships also made regular calls in Kobe, Nagasaki, Shanghai, and Hong Kong.

These first *Empresses* were crack express liners, and in good conditions they could achieve very high speeds of over eighteen knots, with an average sailing speed of sixteen knots. The emphasis on speed and the shorter northern route from Vancouver to Japan allowed these vessels to claim the fastest North American service to the Orient. This record for fast Pacific crossings, combined with the fine yacht-like lines of the vessels and their reputation

for excellent and safe service, made Canadian Pacific's ships very popular among American, Canadian, and British first-class passengers.

Over the years, Canadian Pacific continued to upgrade its Pacific fleet with top-level replacement vessels to keep attracting an upper-class clientele, and this major investment paid off handsomely. Although the main role of the ships was to enhance rail traffic through Canada, the Pacific fleet made money, in both good times and bad, bringing in much-needed revenue for the company. The Pacific *Empress* fleet ended its regular services in January 1941, after fifty years of operation, with the entry of Japan into World War II.

The early *Empresses* could carry up to 900 passengers, 160 of whom were saloon or first class, 40 were second class, and another 600 to 700 were in steerage. Passenger traffic varied tremendously during the year, with the high point in eastbound traffic from the Orient occurring in April, May, and June, and westbound traffic from the West Coast in September, October, and November.

It is important to note that throughout much of the history of the western fleet, the vast majority of its passengers were of Asiatic origin, travelling in steerage to the New World to work as manual labourers, and then, in some cases, returning home. Much of this human trade was staged through Hong Kong, and it was vital for the prosperity of both the British colony and the Canadian Pacific Line.

As well, the vast majority of the company's Pacific crews were made up of Chinese labourers. After 1915, this cheaper labour gave the Canadian ships a great advantage over their American competitors, as union pressure forced American lines to give up this practice.

Canadian Pacific's vessels also carried high-value cargoes of silk, tea, and opium. In spite of tremendous American competition, Canadian Pacific's fast regular schedule allowed it, in the early years, to carry a relatively high percentage of the overall North American trade in these luxury goods. Upon the cargo's arrival in Vancouver, the company sped it across Canada in special trains to what was usually its final destination, the American East Coast.

THE SINEWS OF EMPIRE

The other crucial cargo on board Canadian Pacific's *Empress* fleets was mail. All its first-class, deep-water passenger vessels carried the British mails and were described with the Royal Mail ship prefix, RMS. The Canadian and British governments paid a large subsidy to Canadian Pacific to carry this correspondence to and from the Orient and imposed strict deadlines for delivery, which were backed by heavy financial penalities. Although Canadian Pacific managed for the most part to pocket the subsidy as sheer profit, this revenue sustained the construction and operation of such expensive vessels.

From 1891 to 1906, the company's mail contracts included transport across Canada and the Pacific Ocean but not passage across the Atlantic. With the initiation of its fast Atlantic *Empresses* in 1906, however, the contracts extended right to the United Kingdom.

During the summer months, the mail landed downstream from Quebec City at Rimouski and at Halifax, Nova Scotia, or Saint John, New Brunswick, in the winter months.

It was then loaded on express trains and speeded across the continent to Vancouver, where it was transferred on board the Pacific *Empresses* to depart for Yokohama, Shanghai, and, lastly, Hong Kong. All this high-pressure scheduling required tremendous coordination and was often delayed by ocean storms and the floods, snowstorms, and landslides that regularly occurred along the transcontinental rail system. In spite of these challenges,

Clockwise from far left:

The *Empress of India*'s crew, c. 1890

Empress of India promenade deck with passengers and crew, looking aft from the entrance to the grand saloon

Chinese steerage passengers on board a CP vessel

A hand-painted disposable Japanese tea chest produced for Canadian Pacific

Overleaf: Imperial Federation (British Empire) map of the world from the *Graphic*, July 24, 1886

FREEDOM

FR

GREENLAND

BAFFIN
BAY

DAVIS

STRAIT

HUDSON
BAY

DOMINION OF CANADA

NORTH

NORTH

BRITISH
ISLAND

BERING
SEA

BRITISH
COLUMBIA

VANCOUVER

VICTORIA

NEWFOUNDLAND

NORTH

AMERICA

ATLANTI

San Francisco

PACIFIC

New Orleans

OCEAN

Tropic of Cancer

GULF OF MEXICO

OCEAN

BERMUDA

WEST INDIA
ISLANDS

CAPE VERDE IS

SIERRA
LEONE

JAMAICA

CARIBBEAN SEA

BARBADOES
GRENADA
TRINIDAD

BRITISH
GUIANA

Tropic of Capricorn

SOUTH

SOUTH

PACIFIC

AMERICA

SU

OCEAN

ATLA

FALKLAND IS

S GEORGIA

WC

IMPERIAL FEDERATION,—MAP OF THE W
STATISTICAL INFORMATION FURNISHED BY CAPTAIN

British North America.	1851.	Present Time. Latest Returns
Area	Square Miles	3,519,603
Population	3,471,397	4,604,819
Total Trade Imports	£ 7,906,781	50,586,657
Exports	5,181,441	50,160,969
Shipping, End. & Clrd. tons	3,284,693	9,911,056
Imports from the United Kingdom, 1851		£9,300,607
	present time	7,684,009
Exports to	1851	3,197,607
	present time	9,309,434

British West Indies.	1851.	Present Time. Latest Returns
Area	Square Miles	109,717
Population	966,717	1,806,706
Total Trade Imports	£ 4,720,085	5,802,262
Exports	4,900,063	9,439,353
Shipping, End. & Clrd. tons	1,075,199	6,458,398
Imports from the United Kingdom, 1851		£3,760,008
	present time	4,010,649
Exports to	1851	5,081,772
	present time	4,496,004

FEDERATION

MAP OF THE WORLD.
SHOWING THE EXTENT OF THE BRITISH TERRITORIES IN 1786.

India, Ceylon and Straits.		1861.	Present Time. Latest Returns
Area	Square Miles		960,161
Population		179,687,148	263,970,982
Total Trade	Imports, £	17,909,046	91,044,971
	Exports, £	30,111,916	100,436,887
Shipping, Knld.& Clrd. tons		3,060,809	11,104,087
Imports from the United Kingdom, 1861			39,080,003
	present time		34,436,027
Exports to	1861		4,909,000
	present time		45,809,000

Australasia.		1861.	Present Time. Latest Returns
Area	Square Miles		3,161,949
Population		564,758	3,381,768
Total Trade	Imports, £	4,308,866	94,080,190
	Exports, £	4,306,719	84,579,746
Shipping, Knld.& Clrd. tons		1,962,800	13,361,009
Imports from the United Kingdom, 1861			23,677,904
	present time		31,972,527
Exports to	1861		8,061,147
	present time		37,061,197

South Africa.		1861.	Present Time. Latest Returns
	Square Miles		250,400
Area		408,906	1,074,359
Population	Imports, £	1,769,345	6,590,547
Total Trade	Exports, £	978,107	8,140,978
Shipping, Knld.& Clrd. tons		438,000	1,095,684
from the United Kingdom, 1861			21,464,214
	present time		6,384,991
	1861		599,091
	present time		4,552,984

THE HOUSE FLAG OF CANADIAN PACIFIC

William Van Horne, as president of the line, designed Canadian Pacific's checkerboard house flag himself. This tough railway mogul was also an enthusiastic painter and expert collector of Japanese porcelains. According to one of the many legends told about him, he could even identify these porcelains by touch, blindfolded, with his bare toes! But Van Horne also had the common touch. An inveterate poker player and restless traveller, he enjoyed playing cards all night on the trains with his cronies, who were often reporters. On the day of the press conference introducing the new CP flag, one of these reporters cried out, "Mr. Van Horne, this flag must represent three of a kind!" Van Horne simply stared him down and without missing a beat replied, "No! Three of a kind is not a big enough hand for Canadian Pacific. Only a straight flush will do."

CP's transportation system managed to meet its mail deadlines, only incurring its first penalty a full sixteen years after initiation of the subsidy.

The Canadian vessels travelled west as far as Hong Kong, where the Royal Mail ships of the famous Peninsular and Orient (P&O) Line, travelling east from the United Kingdom via the Suez Canal, met them. In the early days, P&O took approximately thirty-three days, and Canadian Pacific thirty-six, to travel close to 18,000 kilometres (11,000 miles) from the United Kingdom and deliver mail to the colony. Together the two companies straddled the world and provided vital links in the communications system of the British Empire. These were "the sinews of Empire," and they offered the traveller a viable means to beat Jules Verne's *Around the World in 80 Days*, published only four years after the completion of the first American transcontinental railway made such a trip theoretically possible.

Clockwise from left:

The *Empress of India* and the red checkerboard flag, or "red duster," the house flag of Canadian Pacific's fleets. The flag's style allowed for easy identification in calm weather.

P&O *Strathnaver*

P&O SS *Ranci*

Overleaf: Winnipeg market and city hall, c. 1913

BUILDING THE CANADIAN WEST

William Van Horne's prognosis of a straight flush for Canadian Pacific proved correct. In 1911, Canadian Pacific officially owned and operated sixty-five vessels on the world's oceans and the waters of Canada. With the massive pre-war expansion of its Altantic fleet (including the eighteen vessels of the Allen Line, purchased "secretly" in 1909), that number reached nearly one hundred vessels by 1914, making the company the owner and operator of one of the greatest commercial steam fleets ever assembled in the history of navigation.

The company finally matched its Pacific *Empress*-class fleet, initiated in 1891, with a similar passenger service on the Atlantic in 1906, thus fulfilling George Stephen and William Van Horne's dream of fast first-class "through" service from the United Kingdom to the Orient via Canada.

The tremendous expansion of company shipping was linked to the large numbers of immigrants coming to Canada during this period. By the 1890s, good land in the United States had become expensive, and the eyes of the world turned to Canada, one of the last great agricultural frontiers still offering free land to settlers. Between 1896 and 1914, over three million immigrants came to Canada, one million of them settling on the Canadian prairies. Many of them travelled with Canadian Pacific, by water and land, to reach their new homes.

But Canadian Pacific did much more than simply transport immigrants to the West. The company set up numerous company recruiting offices across Europe, and its immigration agents scoured the continent for potential settlers. The company's publicity offices produced millions of guidebooks, booklets, and posters promoting the Canadian West. The scale of CP's promotional operations was so large that the company seemed to be vying with Canada's Department of Immigration for the role of nation builder.

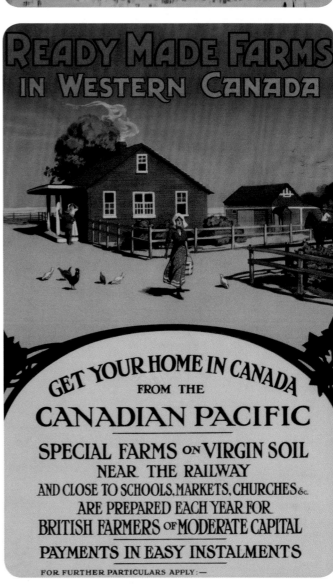

Top: Canadian Pacific settlement poster, c. 1920s

Bottom: Ready-made farms. Canadian Pacific poster, c. 1920

Facing page: Britishers Bring Your Families to Canada — Only $15.00. Canadian Pacific poster, c. 1923

Pages 40-41: A Canadian Pacific poster showing the sixty-five steam vessels officially owned and operated by Canadian Pacific in 1911

BRITISHERS!
BRING YOUR FAMILIES TO CANADA

ONLY **$15.00** 3RD CLASS OCEAN FARE

CHILDREN UNDER 17 YEARS FREE

CANADIAN PACIFIC STEAMSHIPS

ATLANTIC SERVICE

1 EMPRESS OF BRITAIN
2 EMPRESS OF IRELAND
3 LAKE MANITOBA
4 LAKE ERIE
5 LAKE CHAMPLAIN
6 MOUNT ROYAL
7 LAKE MICHIGAN
8 MOUNT TEMPLE

9 MONTFORT
10 MONTCALM
11 MONTROSE
12 MONTEZUMA
13 MILWAUKEE
14 MONMOUTH
15 MONTREAL
16 CRUIZER

PACIFIC SERVICE

17 EMPRESS OF INDIA
18 EMPRESS OF JAPAN
19 EMPRESS OF CHINA
20 MONTEAGLE

UPPER LAKE SERVICE

21 KEEWATIN
22 ASSINIBOIA
23 MANITOBA
24 ATHABASCA
25 ALBERTA

BRITISH COLUMBIA
COAST SERVICE

26 PRINCESS CHARLOTTE
27 PRINCESS VICTORIA
28 PRINCESS MARY
29 PRINCESS ROYAL
30 JOAN
31 CHARMER
32 PRINCESS BEATRICE

CANADIAN PACIFIC RAILWAY CO'S.
STEAMSHIP FLEETS

33 PRINCESS MAY
34 AMUR
35 PRINCESS ADELAIDE
36 TEES
37 CZAR
38 NANOOSE
39 TRANSFER BARGE Nº1
40 TRANSFER BARGE Nº2
41 PRINCESS ENA
42 OTTER

43 QUEEN CITY
44 CITY OF NANAIMO
45 BEAVER
  BRITISH COLUMBIA
  LAKE & RIVER SERVICE
  —
46 HOSMER
47 MINTO
48 SANDON
49 MOYIE

50 YMIR
51 KOKANEE
52 KUSHANOOK
53 OKANAGAN
54 KOOTENAY
55 ROSSLAND
56 ABERDEEN
57 SLOCAN
58 NELSON
59 COLUMBIA

60 PROCTOR
61 YORK
62 WHATSHAN
63 VALHALLA

  FERRY SERVICE
64 ONTARIO
65 MICHIGAN

Canadian Pacific agents were especially active in the United Kingdom and by 1900 had saturated the British market in their search for potential immigrants. In London, the company's offices, and those of the Canadian government, were located in the heart of the metropolis, near the entrances to some of the city's busiest underground stations. Their windows literally displayed the advantages of life in Canada to hundreds of thousands of British citizens. All told, 1.8 million Britons left for Canada between 1900 and 1914, representing over 60 percent of the total number of emigrants destined for the dominion during this period.

Although some eleven different lines were involved in the lucrative pre-World War I transportation of immigrants to Canada, Canadian Pacific ultimately controlled the bulk of the trade. From 1909, when the eighteen ships of the Allen Line were added to its own eleven Atlantic passenger-carrying vessels, the company handled over ninety thousand immigrants a year, a figure which included two-thirds of the total number leaving the port of Liverpool, the major point of British departure, for Canada.

The significance of the nineteenth-century wood trade between the two countries made Liverpool Canada's port of entry and exit to and from the United Kingdom. At the turn of the twentieth century, hundreds of thousands of British emigrants, and those from other northern European countries, left from its docks for Canada.

Glasgow with its Clydebank, where most of Canadian Pacific's vessels were built, was also an important point of departure for Canada. The heavy Scottish immigration to Canada in the nineteenth century continued into the twentieth, with over four hundred thousand Scots leaving the old country for Canada between 1901 and World War II. At least half of them headed for the Canadian West.

Above: Glasgow, 1927. Scottish emigrants travelling with Canadian Pacific being piped away for Canada.

Facing page: Liverpool docks with emigrants leaving for Canada, c. 1900–14

Today, out of a total thirty-four million Canadians, almost five million, or some 15 percent, can claim Scottish descent. Brought into service in 1906, the *Empress*-class vessels of Canadian Pacific's Atlantic fleet could carry as many as one thousand immigrants on board. The arrival of the *Empress*es marked a dramatic change in the treatment of those travelling in third class. Increased competition among the lines meant that companies like Canadian Pacific were obliged to accommodate these passengers in cabins with a free bed, pillow, and blanket, instead of in the large dormitories that had been customary. Meals were now served in large mid-ship dining saloons with passengers sitting on individual chairs rather than benches. The food and hygiene were adequate, and though the immigrants were obliged to wash their own dishes, their plates and utensils were provided free of charge.

All of this marked a literal sea change in the immigrant experience, especially with the much shorter passage time that faster ships like the *Empress*es provided. However, the company's Allen Line still used many smaller and slower

vessels in this trade, where conditions were overcrowded, cheap, and substandard. Hundreds of immigrants might be housed in one large room on such vessels, and they shared sleeping, eating, and bathroom facilities. A few days before, the same ship might have been used to house cattle shipped from Canada to Europe. No washing down completely removed the vestiges of their passage before human beings replaced them on the vessel's next western run.

Another element of the immigrant passage was the presence of hundreds of children on board. Besides those belonging to migrant families, these included numerous chaperoned groups of "home" children, orphaned,

Above: Glasgow, 1927. Scottish emigrants departing from the docks

Facing page: A passenger exercises by skipping on board the *Empress of Britain*, 1910.

abandoned, or paupered juveniles who philanthropic organizations in the United Kingdom believed had a chance of a better life in rural Canada. Between 1869 and 1948, over one hundred thousand of them were sent to Canada, their average age ranging between six and fifteen.

When immigrants came up on the forward well deck of vessels like the *Empresses*, the first- and second-class passengers watched them from the decks above. They served as a major amusement and distraction for the upper classes at a time of extreme social divisions. The vessels were thus floating microcosms of the society that built them.

After 1891, Eastern Europeans were actively recruited to Canada. In spite of existing prejudices, Canada desperately needed to attract settlers to its western frontier and these "sheepskin peasants," as they were called, were regarded as hardy settlers and experienced farmers. All told, about 170,000 came to Canada during this period. Most of them were of Slavic origin and came from the Austro-Hungarian provinces of Galacia and Ruethia, the majority of them Ukrainians and Poles. As well, a number of religious minorities were accepted: Mennonites, Hutterites, Doukhobors, and Jews, many of them religious dissenters or refugees from the Russian Empire.

It is interesting to note, however, that ethnic prejudices kept immigrants of Slavic or Southern European origin from travelling on Canadian Pacific's *Empresses*. Immigration on these top-line vessels was restricted to those of British or Scandinavian origin. The company's advertisements for prospective British immigrants on board the *Empresses* emphasized this fact: "No Foreigners Third Class."

When the ships arrived, the immigrants were immediately processed in dockside centres. The procedure involved the most cursory of medical examinations and a verification of the newcomers' financial resources. From 1910, individual immigrants, male or female, had to have twenty-five dollars in addition to the ticket or funds necessary to travel to a predetermined destination in Canada. Heads of families were expected to have between sixty

Clockwise from right:

A Canadian Pacific colonist sleeping car. Canadian Pacific designed the spartan interior to handle the flow of immigrant traffic to the West. Passengers provided their own bedding and cushions.

The Yanaluk Family, a Slavic family from Germany, standing outside the government dockside immigration centre in Quebec City, 1911

American immigrants arrive in southern Alberta from Colorado in 1914. "A Solid Train Load of Settlers for Alberta" in this "Last Best West."

and one hundred dollars. Once processed, the immigrants immediately boarded waiting trains to start the usual four- or five-day journey to the Canadian West. Each train could carry about four hundred immigrants, and in some cases three trains were necessary to handle all the passengers from just one arriving vessel. Most trains left the docks at night.

Canadian Pacific designed a special colonist sleeping car to provide the cheapest possible accommodation for this type of passenger. The car had upper and lower births, but during the day the passengers sat on benches made of wood slats and were obliged to provide or rent their own bedding, eating utensils, and food for the trip. At the rear of the car were toilet facilities and a stove, which was used for both cooking and heating. Ultimately, Canadian Pacific built over a thousand of these cars.

Conditions on board the colonist cars were uncomfortable, with passengers either choking from the dust, heat, and cinders of the summer months or enduring the extreme cold of winter. They were, however, a vast improvement over the dormitory-style cars that preceded them, and most of the passengers appreciated the opportunity to lie down and sleep in a proper berth. They also marvelled at the extraordinary scenery of their new country, especially as the line crossed the Canadian Shield above Lake Superior, with great outcrops of solid granite rock rising above them and the waters of the lake shining directly below.

READY-MADE FARMS: CANADIAN PACIFIC'S UNIQUE CONTRIBUTION

But Canadian Pacific's role did not end with transportation and promotion. Once the settlers arrived in the West, CP not only sold them their land but also provided seed, tools, and the knowledge necessary for the difficult task of northern dryland farming. The company even built houses and barns and broke the prairie sod for a number of British settlers. Over and over again, Canadian Pacific bent over backwards to help settlers successfully establish themselves. All told, the company assisted with the creation some fifty-five thousand farms on the seventeen million acres of land that it ultimately sold. It is true that the company made a good deal of money out of these sales, about $110 million dollars, but it reinvested 90 percent of that in the development of the railway itself. The extent of its efforts to settle the Canadian West was exceptional, if not unique, in North American railway history.

A NEW PRAIRIE CULTURE

By building up the West and bringing together people from different parts of Europe and the United States (over seven hundred thousand Americans came north during the early years of the twentieth century, thanks at least in part to CP's promotional efforts), Canadian Pacific created a new hybrid prairie culture, one with a different way of thinking and behaving. Much of this cultural development was linked to the villages and towns established near the line's railway stations.

Between 1903 and 1912, Canadian Pacific constructed over 9,700 kilometres (6,000 miles) of additional track in the West, most of which were branch lines connecting

the interior countryside to the company's trunk lines. Over eight hundred stations were established along the CP lines, one for almost every 13 kilometres (8 miles) of track. One of Canadian Pacific's first branch lines linked Calgary to Edmonton. Located 90 kilometres (56 miles) north of Calgary, Olds became a stop on the new branch line in 1890, and the connection stimulated the rapid development of the town and its surrounding area. A postcard image created for the community conveys the excitement of this boom period in the West, with its boosterism and the dreams of unlimited development and material well-being.

Along Canadian Pacific's main line, divisional points were set up approximately every 200 kilometres (125 miles) of track to fuel and water the steam locomotives and maintain the tracks. These divisional points are still used today to organize the operation of the line.

Large towns often sprang up at these divisional points, the biggest being Winnipeg, the "Gateway to the West." It was through Winnipeg that the majority of the immigrants flowed west, and in turn, the town became the main distribution point of goods for Western Canada and handled

———

Olds, Alberta, c. 1916

enormous amounts of prairie grain on its way to eastern markets. By 1903, Winnipeg boosters claimed that the city received more grain per day than Chicago, Minneapolis, and Duluth combined, and that its rail yards, with 125 miles of track, were the largest in the world!

THE PINNACLE OF POWER

By the end of World War I, Canada had become the world's leading grain exporter, its western settlement was well advanced, and it seemed well on its way to fulfilling Sir Wilfrid Laurier's prediction that the twentieth century would be Canada's. The success of this western development was an extraordinary achievement for such a young country, especially as it came about in such a short period of time.

Canadian Pacific perfectly mirrored Canada's success and optimism. By 1913, although two other railway companies, the Grand Trunk Pacific and the Canadian Northern, had developed extensive rail networks on the Canadian prairies, Canadian Pacific still controlled the bulk of traffic, with over half of the thirteen thousand miles of existing western track. With its ships and trains, mines and smelters, thirteen million acres of land still for sale in the West, and eighteen magnificent hotels, the company reached the pinnacle of its power.

A portion of Winnipeg Freight yards. The largest in the world

Above: The Winnipeg freight yards after 1900

Left: "Opening of Navigation at Port Arthur, Ontario, May 2, 1912." The CP and Canadian Northern Railway dockyards on Thunder Bay, Lake Superior, and the departure of twenty vessels carrying a record-breaking five million bushels of western grain to eastern Canada. A long opening has been cut in the ice to allow the ships to leave the harbour.

Overleaf: CPR general superintendent Harry Abbott (standing) accompanies the Governor General of Canada, Lord Stanley, and his party on a locomotive cowcatcher in 1889. William Van Horne is at the far left, with crew members and railway officials.

51

EARLY TRANSCONTINENTAL TRAIN TRAVEL

William Van Horne's ambitions for Canadian Pacific went well beyond simply handling dusty grain and colonists on its trains. He knew that promoting the unparalleled splendour of the Rocky Mountains would also attract tourists to use the line, and by doing so, he started the development of international tourism on a major scale in Canada. To stimulate the imagination of potential travellers, Van Horne sent out dozens of artists and photographers to capture the beauty of the Rockies, using their works as illustrations for an enormous publicity campaign in Europe and the United States.

As an artist himself, Van Horne personally oversaw much of the endeavour to create illustrations of the mountain scenery for the company's first tourist brochures. And often, after inspecting the artists' work, he would tell the painters to go back and make the mountains bigger and the trains smaller!

Van Horne was probably also directly involved in the writing of the text that accompanied these brochures. Here is an example that describes the mountain scenery along the tracks in the precipitous canyon of the Fraser River:

> Hundreds of feet above the river is the railway, notched into the face of the cliffs, now and then crossing a great chasm by a tall viaduct or disappearing in a tunnel through a projecting spur of rock, but so well made, and so thoroughly protected everywhere, that we feel no sense of danger. For hours we are deafened by the roar of the water below and pray for the broad sunshine once more. The scene is fascinating in its terror, and we finally leave it gladly, yet regretfully.

In spite of the visual and literary exaggeration that sometimes accompanied his promotional material, Van Horne succeeded in relaying to the world a positive message about Canada, a message which today is still part of the country's international image: "a land of extraordinary natural wonders, great cultural diversity, and unlimited potential."

The Challenge of the Mountain

Frederick Marlett Bell-Smith, a Canadian born in Great Britain (1846–1923), was one of the artists who took advantage of the free travel passes Van Horne offered to sketch and paint the Canadian West. His work offered a romantic and picturesque vision of the grandiose scenery of the foothills of the Rocky Mountains near Banff and of the Native inhabitants, the Stoney Nakoda Nation. It was exactly this kind of wilderness perspective that enticed visitors to travel to the unspoiled western areas of North America.

THE UPPER-CLASS ENGLISH TRAVELLER

The early brochures often made a strong pitch to the upper-class English traveller with a love of empire, picturesque and exotic landscapes, sporting activities, and the spirit of adventure. The following quotation from an early Canadian Pacific brochure reads like a checklist of everything that might appeal to the English aristocrat with time to spare and a desire for novel experiences:

Clockwise from left:

"The Battle of the Rocks." The impact of Van Horne's influence and spirit can readily be seen in the work of John Innes.

"Annie and the Mountains." An early Canadian Pacific poster used to entice mountain climbers to the Canadian Rockies.

"Stoney Nation camp near Canmore, NWT, 1899," painted by Frederick Marlett Bell-Smith

Overleaf: CP posters, 1912: "Fishing and Shooting" by Philip R. Goodwin; grizzly by Carl Rungius

FISHING AND SHOOTING

CANADIAN PACIFIC RAILWAY

May I not tempt you, kind reader, to leave England for a few short weeks and journey with us across that broad land, the beauties and glories of which have only been brought recently within our reach? There will be no hardships to endure, no difficulties to overcome, and no dangers or annoyances whatever. You shall see mighty rivers, vast forest, boundless plains, stupendous mountains and wonders innumerable, and you shall see all in comfort, nay in luxury. If you are a jaded tourist, sick of Old World scenes and smells, you will find everything fresh and novel. If you are a sportsman, you will meet with unlimited opportunities and endless variety, and no one shall deny you your right to hunt or fish at your sweet will. If you are a mountain climber, you shall have cliffs and peaks and glaciers worthy of your alpenstock, and if you have lived in India, and tiger hunting has lost its zest, a Rocky Mountain grizzly bear will renew your interest in life.

You want big game—stately elk, fierce bears, sneaky panthers, big-horned sheep, snowy goats, etc.? Very good. You can have them one and all, and caribou and deer to boot, providing you yourself are game to follow the guide. The pursuit of what is generally dubbed by the craft "big game" in the mountain wilds of Canada is no child's play. To be successful, a man must possess iron nerve and unflinching determination; he must be a good shot, and strong enough to stand the rough work; for the latter is frequently necessary before the game can be reached, and the former is very liable to be an extremely useful accomplishment, especially if the quarry happens to be a grizzly bear....

Shooting the grizzly is other work. The big plantigrade is always looking for trouble, and when he digs up the hatchet he goes on the warpath. You will have no friendly elephant, nor army of beaters, to satisfy his craving for somebody's scalp. You start on his track, and follow him into his gloomy fastness amid a chaos of rocks, your life in one hand and your rifle in the other; and unless you are made of the right material, stop before the scent gets too hot, or per adventure you may be found empty handed by your party.

However, this spice of dan—, or rather danger spiced with a chance of escape, is very fascinating; and, if you would fain be fascinated to your heart's content, seek the Rocky Mountains of British Columbia and enjoy your whim.

THE TRANSCONTINENTAL SERVICE

Canadian Pacific's transcontinental service ran 4,688 kilometres (2,906 miles) from Montreal to Vancouver. It initiated service in the spring of 1886, with Atlantic and Pacific expresses leaving daily, except for Sundays, from their respective terminuses. These first expresses ran at an average speed of twenty-one miles per hour and took almost six days to cross the continent. In 1899, a second through-train service was established during the summer months, the Imperial Limited, which cut passage time to just over four days. Ultimately, CPR's transcontinental service would reach its peak during the summer months of the 1920s, with four transcontinental trains departing daily in each direction. Rail historian David Jones quotes a CP brochure of the period that stated: "at 8:00 a.m. each day, 36 transcontinental trains are en route, with 36 dining cars serving breakfast."

Windsor Station, the eastern transcontinental terminus, located in the heart of downtown Montreal, opened in 1889. Designed by American architect Bruce Price in the Romanesque Revival style, it was expanded on several occasions and served as the eastern terminus until 1978, when the company gave up all its passenger services. The building also served as the company's headquarters until 1996, when Canadian Pacific's corporate operations were moved to Calgary, Alberta.

The western terminus of the line was established on the waterfront of Vancouver Harbour in 1886. It was replaced in 1898 with a building designed by the eminent Montreal architect Edward Maxwell and remained in operation until 1914. This second station was constructed with turrets and spires in the Chateau style initially created by the company for the construction of the Chateau Frontenac.

Van Horne was unwilling to give up his first-class passenger revenues to George Pullman's Palace Car Company, which provided luxury railcar service for many of the American lines. Instead, in his expansive manner, Van Horne had his own first-class parlour and sleeping cars designed, which were bigger and more luxurious

than those offered by Pullman. With its usual modesty, the company brochure informed European clients: "the railway carriages to which you are accustomed are dwarfed to meet Old World conditions, but these in our train seem to be proportioned to the length and breadth of the land."

In his book *More Classic Trains*, Arthur Dubin described their equipment: "The new cars were built with exteriors of varnished solid mahogany; interiors were satinwood, inlaid with brass and mother-of-pearl in Japanese designs. Parisian marble lavatories contained fittings of beaten bronze. Clerestory window ventilators were of colored Venetian Glass; upholstery was sea-green plush; floors were covered with Turkey carpets."

Canadian Pacific Imperial Limited Transcontinental Express, early twentieth century

my ship at the wharf.

Buddie

Second-class cars and colonist cars also made up part of the "consists," or cars of Canadian Pacific's early transcontinentals. Initially, the second-class cars were day coaches, with passengers offered the option of sleeping free of charge in the accompanying colonist cars. By the 1890s, increasing demand for middle-class travel obliged the company to create a tourist sleeping car service similar to that of a first-class sleeping car but without all the luxury fittings and at half the price.

In the early years, however, Van Horne could not offer his passengers dining car service in the mountainous regions of the west. These cars were simply too heavy to be used on the steep grades. Instead, three restaurant stops to feed transcontinental travellers were constructed along the line.

Work began on these stops in 1886 at three key locations: Mount Stephen House at Field in the Kicking Horse Valley, Glacier House at the foot of the Illecillewaet Glacier near Rogers Pass, and Fraser Canyon House at North Bend in the Fraser River Canyon. Constructed evocatively in the style of a Swiss chalet, these buildings also housed guests. They were the first of Canadian Pacific's famous picturesque resorts and hotels and quickly became popular destinations in their own right. Sadly, all three of these early hotels were later demolished.

If the expectations created by Canadian Pacific's brochures were great, so were the many problems that the line faced in the early days. Canadian Pacific's main track had been built so quickly that it was only partially ballasted, and travellers compared the ride to the pitching and rolling of a ship during a winter storm on the Atlantic. The natural dangers of avalanches, forest fires, and snowstorms in the mountains combined with the rough track, and some of Canadian Pacific's early travellers were actually stranded for weeks along the line.

Clockwise from above:

An early Canadian Pacific dining car

Interior of a CPR first-class sleeping car, c. 1910

View at Mount Stephen, Field, BC, summit of the Rocky Mountains. *Illustrated London News*, 1899

Facing page, top to bottom:

Windsor Station, Montreal, headquarters of the CPR, c. 1900

Canadian Pacific Railway terminus, Vancouver, c. 1900. One of the company's white *Empress*es, offering transcontinental rail passengers "through" service to the Orient, is docked below the station. The inscription on the postcard reads: "my ship at this wharf … Buddie."

Mount Stephen House, Field, BC, c. 1909

A TRANS-SHIPMENT

Edward Roper, an English artist and writer, travelled by rail with the CPR through the mountains in the spring of 1887 and described his misadventures in his book *By Track and Trail*. Arriving in the mountains during a driving snowstorm, Roper and his fellow passengers were obliged to abandon their train near Banff and cross the Bow River by foot, over a trestle bridge 366 metres (1,200 feet) long, walking on sleepers that were eighteen inches apart.

> At the present moment the track was twisted out of form by the accumulation of ice and logs piled against the upper side. The roadway was something like eighteen feet above the raging torrent, and was wet and slippery with half-melted snow, while there was blowing a hard, cold gale. Across this shaky scaffolding we were all told we must walk, and carry our goods.... I shall not easily forget that mauvaise quart d'heure."

Later, while crossing through the Kicking Horse Pass, a rock slide almost knocked Roper's train car off the tracks and down into the rushing river below:

> For a stone as big as a man's head came crashing through a window of the car.... Then we heard stones pouring down the mountain-side on our left, thundering against the wheels of our car, and bombarding the side of it. For some moments the sounds were appalling. Terror was visible in every face.

Another major hazard of rail travel during this period was the fires that the flying sparks of the railway engines often started. After safely passing through the avalanche in the Kicking Horse Pass, Roper's train encountered one of these fires in the Kicking Horse Canyon:

> We ascended a little, and came into the densely wooded country. But oh! What a forlorn, what a miserable, desolate scene! All around us stretched miles of burnt and still burning woods. Everything was black and scorched, not a green thing left, nothing besides bare black trees and logs, grim rocks, and snow-topped mountains! The smoke hung heavily

Glacier House, transcontinental train, and Great Asulkan Glacier, early twentieth century

about once beautiful valleys, where the fire was still raging. Burnt logs, burnt trees, charred and smoking ruin, met our eyes on every side. The telegraph poles were in flames here and there, and the bridges we crossed were only saved from destruction by the utmost exertions of the "section men," who are stationed in gangs along the line to protect them.

Further on in the Selkirk Mountains, near the famous Loops, heavy snowfall delayed Roper's train for several days, and the passengers were obliged to put up at the company's Glacier House. It had been a momentous trip, to say the least, demonstrating all the potential hazards of early train travel in the Rockies, and it resulted in a much-delayed arrival in Vancouver. One imagines that the travellers were glad to get off the train in one piece.

SNOWSHEDS

After the completion of the main line in 1885, Canadian Pacific quickly moved to upgrade its infrastructure, increase its operating efficiency, and better ensure the safety of its passengers. One of the company's main efforts was the construction of dozens of enormous snowsheds. These sheds were placed in key areas where snow slides or avalanches were likely to occur, thus facilitating the running of the trains through the mountains, especially during the extremely difficult winter months.

Thirty of these snowsheds were constructed over a five-mile stretch in the Selkirk Mountains, in the vicinity of the Loops in Rogers Pass. The pass was caught in the snow shadow of the mountains, and as much as forty feet of snow could pile up in the winter months, obliging the company to build structures that could withstand enormous pressures and weights.

ONE OF THE WORLD'S GREAT RAILWAY JOURNEYS

With an upgraded line and Van Horne's publicity campaign, CPR's ride through the Rocky Mountains soon became known as one of the world's great train journeys. Although actual traffic figures for this early period are unknown, rail travel through the mountains grew steadily on the CPR during the 1890s as the company put Canada "on the main line of international rail travel."

And at least one traveller was impressed at the cosmopolitan character of the travellers:

One day a gentleman gave us a long description of the railway system in India and of the license laws in New Zealand. We had descriptions of Bismarck, the deceased Emperors, the present Emperor and Von Moltke from a German gentleman who might as well have passed himself off as Bismarck's brother. We had chats about sleighing in Northern Russia, about sunsets in Norway, and bush life in Australia, and one

would fancy that England, France, Germany, Japan and China were stations on the road, one heard so much about them.

Adolph de Meyer was a photographer famed for his elegant photographic portraits in the early twentieth century, many of which depicted the leading celebrities of the day. His wife, Olga, was a British-born artist's model, socialite,

_____

Clockwise from left:

Snowsheds and loop in the Selkirk Mountains near Rogers Pass

Snowshed construction in the Selkirk Mountains, c. 1886

Summer and winter tracks near Glacier, Glacier Park, BC, 1897

patron of the arts, writer, and fashion figure. A muse for many of the greatest painters of her day, she was also rumoured to be the natural daughter of King Edward VII.

One of the great perks for VIP travellers, such as Lord Stanley, governor general of Canada from 1888 to 1893, was the possibility of a breathtaking ride through the mountains on the locomotive's cowcatcher.

Another beneficiary of the cowcatcher was Lady Agnes Macdonald, the wife of Sir John A. Macdonald, Canada's first prime minister. Macdonald's ardent support of Canadian Pacific was crucial for the line's successful completion, and the company owed him and his Conservative Party VIP treatment.

Prime Minister Macdonald was a colourful character, and his wife's excesses matched his. To the stunned surprise of Canadian Pacific officials, during her trip on the line in the fall of 1886, she decided to ride alone on the cowcatcher from the Rocky Mountains all the way to Vancouver, a distance of over 800 kilometres (500 miles). The following year, she published a description of her descent into the Kicking Horse Pass in an article titled "By Cow and Cowcatcher."

Another moment and a strange silence has fallen round us. With steam shut off and brakes down, the 60-ton engine, by its own weight and impetus alone, glides into the pass of the Kicking Horse River, and begins a descent of 2,800 feet in twelve miles. We rush onward through the vast valley stretching before us, bristling with lofty forest, dark and deep, that, clinging to the mountainside, are reared up into the sky. The river, widening, grows white with dashing foam, and rushes downwards with tremendous force. Sunlight flashes on glaciers, into gorges, and athwart huge, towering masses of rock crowned with magnificent tree crests that rise all round us of every size and shape. Breathless — almost awe-stricken — but with a wild triumph in my heart, I look from the farthest mountain peak lifted high before me, to the shining pebbles at my feet! Warm wind rushes past; a thousand sunshine colours dance in the air. With a firm right hand grasping the stanchion, and my feet planted on the buffer beam, there was not a yard of that descent in which I faltered for a moment.... I could only gaze at the glaciers that the mountains held so closely.... and on a hundred rainbows made by the foaming, dashing river, which swirls with tremendous rapidity down the gorge on its way to the Columbia in the valley below. There is a glory of brightness and beauty everywhere, and I laugh aloud on the cowcatcher, just because it is all so delightful!"

Left to right:

Baron and Baroness de Meyer on the CPR in Western Canada, c. 1900

Lady Agnes Macdonald, the wife of the Canadian prime minister
Sir John A. Macdonald, 1868

"Kodaking" the Three Sisters near Canmore, Alberta. Beatrice Longstaff Lance photograph.

THE OTHER TRANSCONTINENTALS

Canadian Pacific always faced tough American competition for both transcontinental passenger traffic and freight coming from the Orient. The United States initiated its first transcontinental with the meeting of Leland Stanford's Central Pacific and the Union Pacific at Promontory Summit in 1869. Numerous other transcontinentals followed, and ultimately five different American lines offered some type of transcontinental service.

In Europe, express trains were first organized on a regular basis by CWIL, La Compagnie Internationale Des Wagons-Lits, a company founded in 1872 by Belgian businessman George Nagelmackers. Nagelmackers initiated the first run of the famous Orient Express in 1883, but political problems delayed rail construction in the Balkans, and the first all-rail trip from Paris via Vienna to Constantinople (Istanbul) started only in 1889.

The construction of Russia's Trans-Siberian began in 1891 and was opened to Vladivostok, via Manchuria, in 1904. From Moscow it covered an approximate distance of 7,860 kilometres (4,884 miles) and took ten days to cross. The Russo-Japanese War delayed regular service until 1907.

ALONG THE LINE OF
THE CANADIAN PACIFIC RAILWAY

A popular pastime for those travelling on Canadian Pacific's train was photography, which by this time had become widely accessible to the general public. George Eastman's Kodak was a very simple box camera with a fixed-focus lens and single shutter speed, and it offered the consumer a relatively low-priced and easily operated apparatus to record their travel experiences. First introduced in 1888, by 1895 the camera had revolutionized the photo industry.

And what did Canadian Pacific's passengers see and talk about in this "brand new" country of Canada and its frontier West? Besides the stunning and grandiose scenery of the country, the conditions and vagaries of on-board train life, and the pleasantries of making new acquaintances, the passengers would have noted the thousands of immigrants pouring into the new agricultural frontier. Although the Canadian West retained over a million new people before World War I, perhaps as many as two million passed through.

Another spectacle for the earliest visitors was the piles of "buffalo" bones heaped up along the line, awaiting shipment to eastern factories. The remnants of one of nature's most extraordinary phenomena, perhaps as many as seventy million bison at one time occupied the North American continent. By 1871, about twelve million of these animals were left on the western plains, but with the arrival of the western railways, they "melted away like snow before a summer rain."

In Canada, the last of the great herds was gone by 1878. They had been killed for their hides, which were used for clothing or industrial purposes, and the remaining bones of the carcasses bleached the prairies white. High in

Above: Loading buffalo bones on board a CP railcar in Saskatchewan, c. 1885

Right: Immigrants on the stairs of Immigrant Hall in Winnipeg, Manitoba, c. 1905

phosphorus, these bones were in turn processed into fer-tilizer and used in the making of buttons and knife handles and to remove impurities and colour from refined sugar.

One of the most fascinating draws for the early visitors in the Canadian West was contact with the region's Native peoples, or First Nations. Southeast of Calgary, the Canadian Pacific Line ran through a reserve of the Blackfoot Nation. Travelling British dignitaries, such as Lord Minto, the governor general of Canada from 1898 to 1904, often visited this reserve, which was within easy access of the railway. To British visitors, the Blackfoot represented another exotic aspect of the far-flung British Empire.

The proud Blackfoot found the transition to sedentary life profoundly difficult. The railway engines of Canadian Pacific frequently ignited fires on the reserve and impeded the tribe's efforts to develop a new economy of ranching and farming. Compensation from the railway for these fires proved very difficult to get.

To earn some kind of income, the Native people sold "buffalo" horns as souvenirs to the passengers when the trains made station stops on the reserve. The horns, although interesting curios, were a powerful symbol of First Nations' decline.

Above: Lord Minto, governor general of Canada, and family with Blackfoot people, September 22, 1900

Left: Blackfoot First Nations women at Gleichen, AB, train station selling "buffalo" horns as tourist souvenirs, c. 1890s

Overleaf: Canadian Pacific tracks cutting across a Blackfoot reserve 80 kilometres (50 miles) southeast of Calgary, c. 1890s

GATEWAY
TO THE ORIENT

William Van Horne was not satisfied with simply building a railway and promoting mountain scenery. He wanted to make the mountains a destination as well as an attraction. In 1883, when workers found several hot springs near the line at Banff, Van Horne decided to build the first of CP's resort properties, the Banff Springs Hotel. The famous New York Gilded Age architect Bruce Price designed the hotel in Scottish Baronial style, and it opened in 1888. Van Horne's objective with Banff was to emulate the great spas of Europe, where the rich travelled for their health as well as for pleasure and took the waters, literally drinking the sulphurous water.

At the same time as the hotel was being built, Van Horne was lobbying the Canadian government for the creation of a national park to attract visitors to the hotel and the rail line. What would become Banff National Park, Canada's first, was initiated in 1885 with the establishment of a nature reserve. The creation of nearby Yoho National Park followed shortly thereafter. The American transcontinental rail lines used exactly the same process to increase tourist traffic in the American West, creating national parks at Yellowstone, Glacier, and the Grand Canyon.

According to legend, the original Banff Springs Hotel was built 180 degrees in the wrong direction, with the kitchen of the hotel facing the extraordinary scenery of the Bow Valley and the Fairholme Range. When Van Horne saw the mistake, his giant temper exploded, and a tea house–gazebo was quickly constructed so that visitors could enjoy the view along with the kitchen staff.

At Quebec a hotel was needed for passengers arriving by ship from Europe. Local Quebec businessmen hoped to beat Van Horne to the punch by building a large hotel in the late 1880s. It was to be located halfway down the cliffs of the upper city and connected to an opera house

---

Below: The Banff Springs Hotel with carriage road to train station, c. 1908

Facing page: Banff Springs Hotel and National Park, Canadian Pacific brochure, 1897

Preceding pages: Canadian Pacific's *Empress of Ireland* docked in Quebec City, with the Chateau Frontenac in the background, c. 1910–14

Canadian National Park

BANFF SPRINGS

Glaciers and Mountain Ranges OF BRITISH COLUMBIA

CANADIAN PACIFIC LINE

Chg toule tous bien Quebec 3/15/08
fasirs des plus sucrés de
Arthur Alcé

W.Jachi

just below. Unfortunately, the individuals involved were not able to complete their financing, and the Fortress Hotel, as it was to be called, was never built.

William Van Horne was not settling for halfway down the cliff and picked one of the most prestigious sites in all of North America, the clifftop perch of the Chateau St. Louis,

for his hotel. Overlooking the majestic St. Lawrence River, the chateau had been the residence of the governors of New France, and later British North America, for over 170 years before burning down in 1834. Bruce Price, the architect who designed the Chateau Frontenac, stated that with such an extraordinary location and history, he

Above: The Chateau Frontenac, c. 1908

Left: Design by Bruce Price for the original Chateau Frontenac, showing the inner courtyard

Facing page: Interior of the first Chateau Frontenac: the lobby of the Riverview Wing

had no choice but to construct the new hotel in a French style. The ghosts and spirits of the site, he stated, guided his hand.

Price chose as his inspiration the Renaissance chateaux of the Loire Valley with their circular towers, steeply pitched roofs, and high dormer windows. These elements created a picturesque effect and gave the Chateau Frontenac a romantic and aristocratic appeal. The building, however, also embodied many Scottish elements, particularly Price's use of light-coloured brick for the outer walls. The resulting mixture of materials and styles appealed to both English and French Canadians and soon became the national style of not only Canadian Pacific but also all of Canada.

The construction of the hotel began in 1892, and Canadian Pacific planned to have the Chateau Frontenac opened in the spring of 1893 for British travellers passing through Canada on their way to the Chicago World's Fair. Unfortunately, due to construction problems, the hotel did not open until December of that year, long after the famous exhibition had ended.

The hotel, with its inspiring silhouette and extraordinary location, immediately proved popular with the travelling public and quickly became a destination in itself. Van Horne himself had boasted that he would make the hotel the most talked about on the continent, and he was not far off.

As the chateau's fame grew, Bruce Price was called back in 1897 to construct an additional wing, the Citadel, which opened in 1899. Another architect, Walter Painter, completed another major addition, the Mont-Carmel Wing, in 1909. With some 330 rooms, this sprawling, castle-like hotel dominated the skyline of the old walled city and soon came to symbolize the very identity of the historic French town.

QUEBEC'S TERCENTENARY CELEBRATIONS

In July 1908, to celebrate the three hundredth anniversary of the founding of the city, three different levels of government organized an extraordinary ten-day spectacle. It included a total of eleven warships from the United Kingdom, France, and the United States, historical pageants played out by hundreds of costumed local citizens, and a march past of thirteen thousand Canadian militia troops. The presence of numerous dignitaries, including the Prince of Wales (the future King George V) and the vice-president of the United States, Charles W. Fairbanks, also enhanced the event. Such a romantic display had never been seen before in Canada —and would never be seen again.

The main focus of the event was the creation of a national park on the site of the British victory over the French in 1759 on the Plains of Abraham. It was hoped that the joint efforts of French and English Canadians to host the celebrations would bring them closer together during a period of rapidly growing national tensions and imperialism.

Through all of this, the Chateau Frontenac played the aristocratic role for which it had been created. It hosted the many dignitaries who came to the celebrations, providing the perfect backdrop for the romantic Edwardian spectacle, and served as a symbol of power and legitimacy for the leaders of this young country, all the while emphazing Canada's strong links with the British Empire.

———

Below: Dufferin Terrace in front of the Chateau Frontenac, during the Quebec tercentenary celebrations, 1908. Eleven large warships dominated the river in front of the city as their sailors walked through the crowds.

Facing page: Quebec tercentenary, July 22, 1908. Awaiting the arrival of the Prince of Wales, the future King George V, approaching the city on board the new British dreadnought *Indomitable*.

CANADIAN PACIFIC'S ATLANTIC FLEET

Because of competition from other Canadian shipping lines on the Atlantic and the problem of finding a suitable winter port—the St. Lawrence River not being navigable during the winter months—Canadian Pacific did not enter the Atlantic shipping trade until 1903. In late 1904, in an effort to capture the existing mail contracts between Canada and the United Kingdom, it ordered the construction of two intermediate-sized liners of high quality, the *Empress of Britain* and the *Empress of Ireland*, to provide eighteen-knot service to Canada. Put into operation in 1906, the *Empresses'* high-speed service allowed them to win these contracts and, when combined with the shorter sailing distance between Europe and Canada, to compete favourably with similar fast vessels on the Liverpool–New York City route.

THE GATEWAY TO THE ORIENT: THE CHATEAU FRONTENAC

During the summer months, Quebec City was the key entry point for Canadian Pacific's travel system in North America, which led to Asia. To emphasize this point, the company's literature proudly presented the Chateau Frontenac as the "Gateway for the new route to the Orient."

Four passenger vessels on the Canada run allowed the company to provide weekly service during the busy summer months. Two of these ships travelled on the St. Lawrence River as far upstream as Montreal. The deeper draught of the new *Empresses*, however, obliged them to stop farther downstream, at Quebec. As a result, boat trains were organized on the day of the *Empresses'* departure to bring their passengers down from Montreal to Quebec City and, in turn, to meet the arrival of the two vessels to speed those who were not staying in the city farther west.

The two *Empresses* operated in tandem on a twenty-one-day, round-trip cycle that included a crossing of approximately six days and an average five-day turnaround in Quebec and Liverpool. The schedules of the *Empress of Britain* and the *Empress of Ireland* often saw them pass one another mid-ocean, sometimes within hailing distance. Each made an average of twelve round trips a year.

RUDYARD KIPLING AND THE ILL-FATED *EMPRESS OF IRELAND*

The *Empress of Ireland* was a fast and luxurious vessel of 14,191 gross register tonnage and a length of 174 metres (570 feet), and could carry over 1,530 passengers: 310 in first class, 470 in second class, 500 in third class, and 250 in steerage. Known as a cheerful and popular vessel, she acquired a snobbish reputation as the elegant way to travel to Canada. The upper works of the *Empress of Ireland* and its almost identical sister ship, the *Empress of Britain*, had been extended to provide space for more luxurious cabins and finely decorated public rooms. Even the company's publicity to attract third-class passengers emphasized a reputation for luxury with slogans such as "Go As Your Betters Go."

During its eight years of service, from 1906 to 1914, the *Empress of Ireland* made 191 successful crossings between the United Kingdom and Canada and carried over 186,000 passengers. Its reputation and that of its sister ship helped Canadian Pacific capture a large portion of the Atlantic passenger trade to and from Canada during the very busy pre-World War I period and successfully compete with ten other lines operating in the "Canada Trade." Passengers also included substantial numbers of American travellers, many coming from the American Midwest.

Numerous dignitaries and celebrities, including English and Japanese nobility, travelled on the *Empress of Ireland*.

Left: Rudyard Kipling by Sir Philip Burne-Jones, 2nd Bt, 1899

Facing page: Atlantic Fleet *Empresses*, Canadian Pacific poster, c. 1930

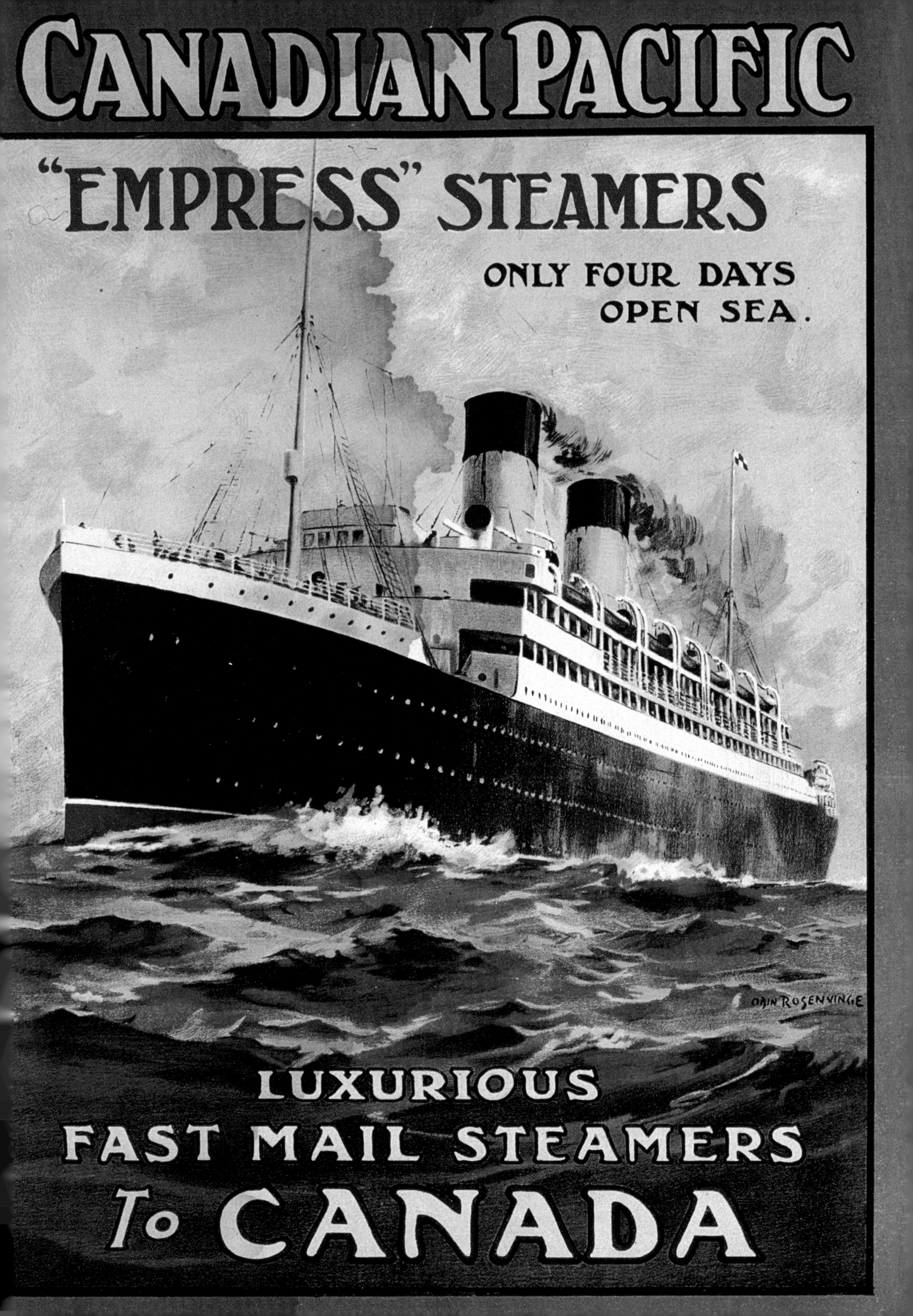
CANADIAN PACIFIC
"EMPRESS" STEAMERS
ONLY FOUR DAYS
OPEN SEA.
LUXURIOUS
FAST MAIL STEAMERS
To CANADA

One of its most famous passengers was Rudyard Kipling, who visited Canada for four weeks in the fall of 1907, several months before he won the Nobel Prize in Literature. Keenly aware of the potential for publicity, William Van Horne organized a special suite with private bath on board the *Empress of Ireland* for Kipling and his entourage and put a private rail car at their disposal for their journey back and forth across the country.

As author Derek Grout notes in his book *Empress of Ireland: The Story of an Edwardian Liner*, Kipling responded favourably to his Canadian Pacific experience in letters later published as "Letters to the Family" in 1910.

Talk about luxury...!

The ship is a wonderful concern. I went all over her with the Captain at Inspection this morning....

A C.P.R. steamer cannot be confused with anything except Canada....

We discussed this [Imperial policy] under the lee of a wet deck-house in mid-Atlantic; man after man cutting in and out of the talk as he sucked at his damp tobacco. The passengers were nearly all unmixed Canadian, mostly born in the Maritime Provinces.... They were at ease, too, among themselves, with that pleasant intimacy that stamps every branch of Our Family and every boat that it uses on its homeward way.... These big men, smoking in the drizzle, had hope in their eyes, belief in their tongues, and strength in their hearts....

The St. Lawrence on the last day of the voyage played up nobly. The maples along its banks had turned blood red and splendid as the banners of lost youth.... A dry wind brought along all the clean smell of their Continent—mixed odours of sawn lumber, virgin earth, and wood-smoke; and they snuffed it, and their eyes softened as they identified point after point along their own beloved river-places where they played and fished and amused themselves in holiday

time.... Understand, they did not in any way boast, shout, squeak, or exclaim, these even-voiced returned men and women. They were simply and unfeignedly glad to see home again, and they said: Isn't it lovely? Don't you think it's beautiful?

We love it.

Tragically, Kipling's beloved *Empress of Ireland* would later sink, in a mere fourteen minutes, on May 29, 1914, in the estuary of the St. Lawrence River, approximately 340 kilometres (210 miles) downstream from Quebec City. The ship collided in thick fog with the Norwegian collier *Storstad*, a vessel whose prow had been reinforced to break through the heavy ice that was often found in the river. The *Storstad*'s prow struck amidship and almost cut the *Empress* in two. The incident occurred at 2:00 a.m., while most of the passengers were sleeping. They had little chance to escape before the vessel sank in the near-freezing waters and swift currents of the river.

Of the 1,477 persons on board, the *Empress of Ireland* suffered 1,012 fatalities, 840 of whom were passengers, a higher loss of passengers than on the *Titanic*. The inquiry that followed held the Norwegian collier responsible for the collision, but grave doubts remained about the actions of the *Empress of Ireland*'s captain, Henry Kendall, during the incident. Although he stayed with Canadian Pacific for most of his long career, he never again commanded one of its vessels.

————

Facing page: Second-class baggage and passengers on board the first *Empress of Britain*, c. 1910

Above: The first-class music room on the *Empress of Ireland*

QUEBEC

CHATEAU FRONTENAC & DUFFERIN TERRACE

CANADIAN PACIFIC RAILWAY

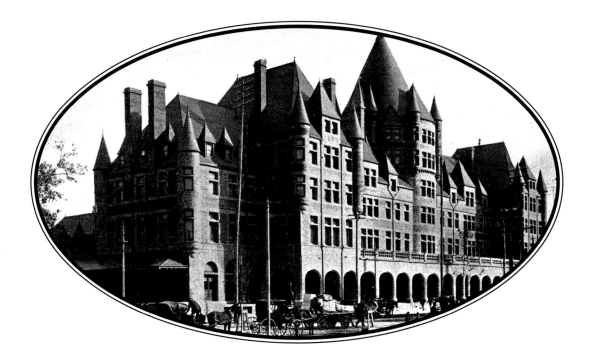

THE CHATEAU STYLE

The whole country soon became dotted with Canadian Pacific's distinctive and luxurious properties. The aristocratic and castle-like appearance of the Chateau style became so popular that competing Canadian railway companies constructed their hotels in similar fashion. All told, ten prominent hotels (five of them Canadian Pacific), numerous railway stations, and many public buildings were built in this style across the country.

Although the Chateau style was not unique to Canada, this architecture so dominated the country that even today no nation in the world is so readily identified by a chain of hotels and its distinctive architecture.

Above: Canadian Pacific's Place Viger railway hotel and station in Montreal, c. 1905. Designed by architect Bruce Price, it opened in 1898.

Below: The Grand Trunk Railway borrowed CP's Chateau style for its Chateau Laurier in Ottawa. Union Station is shown to the right, c. 1912, the year of the chateau's opening. Parliament Hill lies to the left, and train tracks on the raised platform over the Rideau Canal link the hotel complex to the government buildings. The hotel contrasted dramatically with the Classical style of the railway station.

Facing page: Chateau Frontenac, Canadian Pacific poster, c. 1922

EARLY
MOUNTAIN
TOURISM

Canadian Pacific's hotels and mountain resorts were very popular with the travelling public, and by the end of the first decade of the twentieth century they were filled to overflowing in the summer months. Although the hotels did not make large returns for the company on the major fixed investments they required, the chain was crucial as an attraction and convenience that encouraged travellers to patronize the CPR rather than other lines. At the same time, they also provided publicity for the company.

Most of the early tourists who came west to the mountains with the CPR were members of the rising upper-middle class, made rich by the Industrial Revolution. If they were British, they came to see their empire and view its frontiers. Many of them came imbued with the spirit of the great Romantic writers of the nineteenth century—Shelley, Scott, Keats, and Byron—and their search for the sublime through nature. The predecessors of these tourists had found this sensation at Niagara Falls in grand tours of North America, but now, with the railways, the Victorians went farther, to the western mountains, and they went there to be alone with God.

But even if the early visitors went looking for the sublime, they still wanted all the comforts and luxuries that they were used to at home, and this Van Horne was determined to provide. The company's promotional literature emphasized an aristocratic vision of the traveller set against the backdrop of the spectacular mountain scenery and the castle-like hotels. With this perspective, guests always appeared in the company brochures in fine sporting apparel and the frocks and gowns of the upper classes.

The CPR in turn assured that competent guide services were available for visitors. In 1889, Tom Wilson, one of the leading guides, realizing the tourists' fascination with Native people, organized Banff Indian Days with a group of the neighbouring Stoney Nakoda First Nation, in which the Nakoda participated in a series of competitions that exhibited their traditional skills and culture for visitors. Banff Indian Days continued on the grounds of the Banff Springs Hotel for almost ninety years, the last one being held in 1978.

Top: Canadian Pacific Railway Station at Banff, c. 1910–14

Above: The Great Courtyard of the Banff Springs Hotel in the early twentieth century. Surrounded by elegant guests, a Canadian cowboy in chaps represents the exotic nature of a trip to the Canadian West. The image underlined that CP's hotels were the perfect place for well-off travellers to enjoy their travel experience.

Facing page: Woman viewing Mount Temple from across Paradise Valley, c. 1900. This adventuresome woman likely departed from Lake Louise and walked south along a CP hiking trail, for half or three-quarters of the day to enjoy the spectacular view from Saddle Peak.

Preceding pages: Canadian Alpine Club climbing Mount Marpole, 1909

AMERICANS AND THE GREAT CIRCLE ROUTE

Although much of the company's promotion was done in Europe, almost from the start the majority of the visitors to Canadian Pacific's mountain resort hotels were from the American East Coast. Many of these travellers took what was known as the Great Circle Route, travelling by American transcontinental train to the West Coast, with stops in national parks such as Yellowstone, Glacier, and Yosemite (originally a California state park), before cruising north to Alaska. These travellers would often return home via Canada and the CPR. Some of these excursions could take up to two or three months to complete.

Mary Vaux and her brothers, George and William, were among the first American travellers to vacation in the western Canadian mountains, staying at Glacier House in Rogers Pass during the summer of 1887. Members of a highly educated Quaker family from Philadelphia, they fell in love with the Selkirk and Rocky Mountains, coming back on numerous occasions over the next two decades. In 1900, Mary became the first woman to climb Mount Stephen, which towers more than 3,050 metres (10,000 feet) over the Kicking Horse Pass.

Like many of the early repeat travellers to the Rockies, the Vaux family came to study nature as well as to enjoy it. The flora and fauna of the area, the glaciers and the mountains, encouraged scientific study, especially by

groups from major American universities, such as Harvard and Yale. Travel and education were closely linked for these individuals. Mary Vaux, for example, was an expert painter of wildflowers. In 1925, the Smithsonian Institution in Washington, DC, published four hundred of her illustrations as the five-volume *North American Wild Flowers*.

Mary and her brothers were also expert photographers well before the Kodak camera made taking pictures easy for tourists. The necessity of carrying heavy camera equipment up steep mountain peaks involved back-breaking labour, but their efforts created an extraordinary visual record not only of scientific discovery but also of early travel in the western mountains. Today, many of their photos are held in the Vaux collection at the Whyte Museum of the Canadian Rockies in Banff.

Above: "Banff Indian Days." Local Banff residents with members of the Stoney Nation, c. 1910.

Facing page: Visiting Moraine Lake in the Valley of the Ten Peaks, nine miles south of Lake Louise

On one of her many excursions to the Canadian Rockies, Mary Vaux met the paleontologist Charles Doolittle Walcott, secretary (chief executive officer) of the Smithsonian Institution. They married in 1914, when Mary Vaux was fifty-four years old.

Another important early traveller with Canadian Pacific was Mary Schäffer, also a Philadelphia Quaker and a close friend of Mary Vaux. She first visited the area with Vaux in 1889, travelling part of the way on a Canadian Pacific boxcar. Schäffer returned a year later with her new husband, an avid amateur botanist, whom she had met the previous year in the mountains at Glacier House. In 1904, after the sudden deaths of her parents and husband, she returned to the Rockies to find peace of mind and to complete the research for a book on mountain botany that her husband had been writing. A talented artist and photographer, she illustrated and ultimately published the book in 1907.

Mary Schäffer's rugged camping trips in the mountains helped her evolve into a very independent and self-reliant woman. Well known for her wilderness endeavours, she was asked by the Canadian government in 1908 to undertake a survey of Maligne Lake. The lake at that time was a remote body of water, the location of which was known only by the region's Native people, some of whom had visited it many years earlier. Led by the redoubtable and charming guide Billy Warren, Schäffer's group, after tremendous difficulties, found and surveyed the lake. One

Left: Mary and George Vaux on Mount Fairview, overlooking Lake Louise, 1904

Facing page: Mary Vaux with Swiss guide on Illecillewaet Glacier near Glacier House

of the most beautiful sites in all of the Canadian Rockies, the group's work led to the inclusion of Maligne Lake in Jasper National Park, ensuring its protection for future generations.

Schäffer's story had a happy ending. She found personal peace in the Rocky Mountains and settled down in Banff. She married Billy Warren, who was twenty years her junior. Her first husband had been twenty years older. In the end, it all averaged out for Mary Schäffer Warren.

———

Clockwise from above:

Mary Schäffer and guide Billy Warren

Mary Schäffer and guides on a raft making the first recorded exploration of Maligne Lake in the Canadian Rockies, 1908

American visitors in the Selkirk Mountains near Rogers Pass, British Columbia

Picking mountain wildflowers in Yoho National Park, the Canadian Rockies, c. 1920s. Mary Vaux and her friend Mary Schäffer were avid botantists and excellent painters of mountain flowers.

PACIFIC COAST
·TOURS·
THROUGH—THE
CANADIAN
·PACIFIC·
ROCKIES

Above: Canadian Pacific mountain climbing
poster, c. 1917

Facing page: Canadian Pacific Alaska and
British Columbia coast service brochure, 1928

"FIFTY SWITZERLANDS IN ONE"

The demands of sophisticated tourists like the Vaux family and Mary Schäffer Warren motivated Canadian Pacific to provide services for this type of clientele. Its original smaller hotels at Field and Glacier were enlarged and upgraded to provide a more intimate mountain experience than the larger resort hotels, and Swiss guides were hired for those interested in mountain climbing and glacier exploration.

By the 1870s, the last of the great Swiss peaks had been climbed. For those interested in making a first ascent, the closest choices were the Russian Caucasus or the more easily reached Canadian West. Climbing groups from the United States, and Yale University in particular, were especially active in the Canadian Rockies during the 1890s.

Starting in 1899, Canadian Pacific engaged Swiss guides to work to provide a safe and professional guiding service in the Canadian mountains. The company even built a Swiss guide village to house them and their families. Not only did these guides provide an excellent service, but their traditional costumes and style also offered a wonderful publicity opportunity. The company phased out the service in 1955.

Middle-class international tourism began in Switzerland in the 1830s and 1840s, and from Canadian Pacific's start, Van Horne and his advertising machine sought to emulate the success of the Swiss experience by turning the Canadian mountains into the Swiss Alps of North America. The Swiss guides were perhaps the most obvious element of this attempt.

The mountain resorts reached the peak of their potential as early as 1910, when over twenty-two thousand guests stayed at the Banff Springs Hotel. Thousands of other potential guests had to be turned away, and construction on the hotel to expand its facilities continued unabated during this period.

The popularity of the mountain resorts continued through the 1920s and into the 1930s. The upscale clientele of this period could afford to stay for as long as a month at the resorts, and they involved themselves in an intense social whirl of dances, dinner parties, and gala events. These activities centred on the hotels and were known for their elegance and refinement. It was the apogee of the style we now associate with the Golden Age of Travel.

Top: Group of Canadian Pacific Swiss guides

Bottom: Charles Doolittle Walcott, secretary of the Smithsonian Institution, 1907–27. Walcott was also an expert geologist and paleontologist. During one of his many trips to the mountains he discovered one of the world's most important fossil beds of Cambrian life, the Burgess Shale in Yoho National Park, not far from the CPR line at Field, BC.

Facing page: Canadian Pacific brochure, Banff Springs Hotel, c. 1929

Pages 100-101: By 1924, the exterior shell of the new Chateau Frontenac was completed. Image c. 1925.

THE INTERWAR PERIOD

Canadian Pacific's hotels especially prospered in the first years of World War I, American visitors, cut off from Europe, visited the Canadian West in great numbers. With the American entry into the war in 1917, however, tourism fell drastically and did not recover until the end of a post-war depression in 1923. For most of the rest of the decade, the economy flourished and so did Canadian Pacific. Its trains and hotels were filled until the crash of 1929 marked the end of the last golden era of railroad tourism.

During the Roaring Twenties, the company dramatically expanded the capacity of its hotels and resorts. After a major fire in 1926, the two wings of the Banff Springs Hotel were reconstructed in stone around the large central tower. This construction gave the hotel an enlarged capacity of six hundred rooms and created the silhouette for which the building is famous today. The same kind of major expansion would also be undertaken at the nearby Chateau Lake Louise and at the Chateau Frontenac in Quebec City.

Increased competition was also a reality of the 1920s. The new challenge of long-distance car travel, ever-increasing competition offered by the American lines, and the organization, in 1922, of a second Canadian transcontinental giant, the Canadian National Railway, spurred Canadian Pacific to increase the quality and extent of the services it offered its clientele. From new railway rolling stock and ships to the construction of bungalow camps, hiking trails, and tea houses, the company was extremely active during this period.

Left: Banff Springs Hotel in 1929 after the reconstruction, in stone, of the north and south wings of the hotel. The central tower dates from 1914.

Overleaf: Banff Springs Hotel, c. 1935, Canadian Pacific poster

Overleaf, facing page: Chateau Lake Louise, c. 1938, Canadian Pacific poster

A.C. LEIGHTON

Canadian Pacific

CHATEAU LAKE LOUISE
CANADIAN ROCKIES

CHATEAU LAKE LOUISE

During this period, another major area of hotel expansion occurred some thirty miles west of Banff at Lake Louise. One of the most beautiful sites in the Canadian Rockies, Lake Louise lies at the foot of Victoria Glacier and was named for Queen Victoria's fourth daughter, Princess Louise Caroline Alberta, the wife of the Marquess of Lorne, governor general of Canada from 1878 to 1883.

In 1890, a cabin was constructed on the site that contained only two guest bedrooms. It burned down in 1893 and was replaced the next year by a larger structure that, due to the popularity of the site for hikers and mountain climbers, was continuously added on to until World War I.

Clockwise from left:

Chateau Lake Louise with the surviving 1912 wing on the left and the new nine-storey
1925 construction to the right, c. 1928

First Chateau Lake Louise, 1891. Constructed in 1890 and destroyed by fire in 1893

The second Chateau Lake Louise, c. 1920. The building's Tudor-style wings were designed by
the prominent Victoria-based architect Francis Rattenbury and built between 1899 and 1912.

Chateau Lake Louise dining room, c. 1930

In 1924, three of the four pre-war wings of the hotel burned, and in 1925, a nine-storey, 400-room hotel was constructed and linked to the surviving 1913 wing of 350 rooms. In addition, by 1927 over one hundred miles of trails leading from the hotel had been laid out for horseback riding and hiking, with a number of tea houses constructed to provide refreshment along the way.

This was construction on an enormous scale for such a pristine and intimate location. Initially, the site served as a base for more adventuresome and sophisticated visitors, who sought out scientific discovery and mountain exploration. By the 1920s, however, with the arrival of the car, this type of visitor had become less significant for the company, which focused on providing services for a more conventional traveller. The emphasis was now on luxury service, with activities occurring within or close by the hotel.

By the 1920s, the Chateau Lake Louise offered all the glamour and amenities of an upscale resort. The beauty of the location and the monumental design of the hotel, with its vistas and swimming pool, created a profoundly romantic impression and attracted numerous dignitaries and celebrities for holidays or movie shoots. These "stars" included the world's most famous couple of the early 1920s, Canadian-born actress Mary Pickford and her husband, Douglas Fairbanks.

Canadian Pacific added to the western experience it offered by adding open-air observation cars to view the

spectacular scenery along the tracks in the mountain ranges of British Columbia. However, the smoke that rose from the coal-burning steam locomotives, located at both the front and rear of trains in the rougher mountain terrain, played havoc with efforts to view the local scenery. Even a roofed-over observation car was subject to the smoke and cinders of the steam locomotives. Such were the realities of early sightseeing and train travel during the pre-diesel period.

The arrival of long-range western highways changed dramatically the clientele of Canadian Pacific's mountain resorts and hotels. For many visitors, the ability to travel by car became the focal point of their experience. Canadian Pacific constructed a network of bungalow camps to meet the new demand for cheaper accommodation over shorter periods. At the same time, the company's existing network of trails and tea houses was expanded within Banff and Yoho National Parks to enhance opportunities for hiking and trail riding for this new type of clientele.

————

Below: Mountain observation car, 1933

Facing page: Banff Springs Hotel, 1924. The beauty of the natural setting enhanced the castle-like hotel's elegance and fine service.

A KEEP FOR A CASTLE:
A NEW CHATEAU FRONTENAC

In 1919, Canadian Pacific initiated a major expansion of its Quebec City hotel, the Chateau Frontenac. The St. Louis Wing was built to house the hotel's Salle de Bal (ballroom), while the service wing (western side) of Bruce Price's original hotel of 1893 was dismantled to allow the construction of a seventeen-storey central tower. This tower, or keep, enhanced the Chateau Frontenac's already extraordinary profile and made it not only a landmark for the city of Quebec but also a powerful symbol for the whole of Canadian Pacific's travel empire. The new construction was completed by 1924 and brought the total capacity of the Chateau Frontenac to 658 rooms.

The two men responsible for the hotel's expansion were the brothers Edward and William Maxwell of Montreal, two of Canada's finest architects and masters of the use of French Classicism. The elegance and sophistication of their design, with its attention to the detail of the interior decoration, helped create an extraordinarily romantic and beautiful structure. To complete their achievement, Edward Maxwell scoured Europe to find antique furniture that would match the romantic elegance of the building.

Clockwise from below:

The Chateau Frontenac, c. 1910, with the new Mount Carmel Wing on the left, the Citadel Wing in the Centre (1899), and the original Riverview Wing on the far right (1893)

The initial phase of the Chateau Frontenac's 1920s expansion as viewed from the Place d'Armes in February of 1921. On the right, under construction, is the new St. Louis Wing. Visible behind the St. Louis Wing is the high tower of the Mount Carmel Wing, completed in 1909, and to the left, the original 1893 hotel.

By March of 1922, the western, or service wing, of Bruce Price's 1893 hotel had been demolished, and work was started on the foundations of the central tower. Visible in the rear is the remaining Riverview Wing of 1893 and the main entrance to the original hotel.

The burned Riverview Wing, January 16, 1926

Historical touches and French references were everywhere. For the double staircase in the main lobby, which led up to the Palm Room and the hotel's new ballroom, the Maxwells took inspiration from the principal staircase of Madame de Pompadour's palace at Versailles, le Petit Trianon. The Jacques Cartier Room was designed to represent the cabin of *La Grand Hermine*, the ship of Jacques Cartier, the first French explorer to arrive at Quebec. The Maxwells filled the room with historical objects and decorative elements to evoke Quebec's early French history.

English influences were also apparent — this was still the British Empire, after all. Afternoon tea was served each day in the Palm Room, located just outside the entrance to the ballroom. Costumed musicians with powdered wigs played classical music during the service, and when a young woman of local society was invited to attend, it was the equivalent of her "coming out" in Quebec society. This style of tea service underlined the aristocratic tone of the hotel and continued until the 1960s.

Clockwise from below:

Tea in the Palm Room, 1924

Jacques Cartier Room, 1945

The new lobby of the Chateau Frontenac with its coffered ceiling and classical sense of proportion, 1925. Typical of the period was the use of plants to provide decoration and a sense of privacy for the guests.

The main lobby staircase, 1925

Chateau Frontenac, the Dutch Suite, 1924. From the beginning, the Chateau Frontenac promoted its historic links by the decoration of special historic suites, often located in its tower rooms. The Habitant Suite paid tribute to the local French Canadian setting, the Dutch Suite to William Van Horne's own ancestry, and the Chinese Suite to celebrate the CPR's new service to the Orient.

The reading room of the reconstructed Riverview Wing, 1926. Travellers wrote and received letters regularly as they travelled. The tower reading room's desks and natural lighting made it the perfect place to deal with one's correspondence. Today, this space serves as a bar.

In January of 1926, a fire broke out in the Riverview Wing, the remaining wing of the 1893 hotel, and completely destroyed it. William Maxwell, along with the British-born master craftsmen who had worked on the hotel's expansion, was brought back to redo the burned section. Working night and day, they were miraculously able to reconstruct the wing within four months for the upcoming summer season.

During the interwar period, the hotel hosted many of the world's most famous dignitaries and celebrities. These included a number of heroes of the First World War: French marshals Émile Fayolle and Ferdinand Foch, and Baron Byng, who distinguished himself as commander of the Canadian Corps at the Battle of Vimy Ridge. Charles Lindbergh landed on the Plains of Abraham in Quebec City in April 1928 before checking in at the Chateau Frontenac. In 1927, he had become world famous as the first man to fly solo across the Atlantic non-stop, and a year later he flew to Quebec to bring life-giving serum to a sick friend.

Also in the early twenties, Barbara La Marr, a famous actress and screenwriter of the silent film era, shot a film at the Chateau Frontenac. She stunned the staff with her vivacious and alluring personality. She was billed as "the girl who is too beautiful." Unfortunately, the adage proved too

true. She died in 1926, at the age of twenty-nine, having been married five times.

With the expansion of the hotel in the mid-1920s, the Chateau Frontenac decided to organize a week of winter sporting events to attract visitors from Canada and the United States. Activities included ski jumping, skating, snowshoe races, and a dog sled competition that saw teams coming to participate from as far away as Alaska. The week ended with a costumed "dog derby ball" in the hotel. Today the chateau maintains its winter traditions when it hosts the Quebec International Bonspiel, which sees hundreds of curlers staying at the hotel, some coming from as far away as Texas and Japan. The first of these international bonspiels was held in the city in 1913.

––––––––

Below left: Barbara La Marr, c. 1920

Below right: Canadian Pacific ski poster, 1938

Facing page: Chateau skating rink, 1945

THE ROMANCE OF THE ORIENT

The same interwar expansion would also hold true for Canadian Pacific's shipping operations. The company had lost twenty-three vessels during the First World War, twelve by enemy action, the others by accident or sale to the British Admiralty. The company responded to these losses with an extraordinary building and buying program that saw twenty-two passenger ships and freighters added to its various fleets between 1919 and 1931.

In the Pacific, larger and more modern vessels gradually replaced the original *Empresses*. The *Empress of Russia* and the *Empress of Asia* had been brought into operation just before the war, and in 1922 the *Empress of Scotland* and the *Empress of Canada* joined them. With a service speed of eighteen knots, the 199-metre-long (653-foot) *Empress of Canada* was by far the fastest and largest passenger vessel on the Pacific during this period. Finally, in 1930, a new *Empress of Japan* replaced the valiant original vessel of this name, taken out of service in 1922. The first *Japan* had provided an amazing thirty-one years of faithful service for the company and had steamed over 4 million kilometres (2.5 million miles), making 315 crossings of the Pacific Ocean.

The newer vessels allowed Canadian Pacific to offer a fortnightly service to the Orient, and cut passage time between Yokohama and Victoria, British Columbia, to just under nine days. Faster trains and ships reduced the time of mail service from the United Kingdom to Hong Kong from the original thirty-six days of the early 1890s to twenty-nine days by 1906. This increased speed allowed the company to extend its service to Hawaii and the Philippines and to attract a large first-class clientele for the company, while maintaining its competitive position for the carrying of

———

Below: Canadian Pacific's second *Empress of Japan* departing Vancouver, January 2, 1932

Facing page, top: The *Empress of Japan* departing Vancouver, with the Canadian Rugby Union tour to Japan, January 2, 1932

Facing page, bottom: The *Empress of Russia* undergoing a refit at the Kowloon dry docks, Hong Kong, c. 1930

luxury goods. The Pacific fleet remained very profitable for the company, up until the crash of 1929. The enormous distances covered by Canadian Pacific's western fleet must be put into perspective. A voyage from Vancouver to Honolulu and then to Japan, China, and the Philippines covered a distance of 15,657 kilometres (8,454 nautical miles) in one direction, whereas a crossing of the Atlantic involved only 4,000 kilometres (2,146 nautical miles). Vessels like the *Empress of Russia* often travelled as much as 154,000 kilometres (83,500 nautical miles) a year, with much of the distance steamed over the stormy northerly latitudes of the Pacific. These were undertakings of heroic proportions.

In January 1932, a rugby tour was organized between the Canadian and Japanese Rugby Unions, and the Canadian team travelled to Japan on the company's second *Empress of Japan*. Rugby had become very popular in Japan, and the Canadian tour attracted enormous attention. Canada won the first five matches before being defeated 38–5 by the Japanese national team in the final game. Twenty-five thousand spectators were in attendance for the final, including many members of the Japanese royal family.

Canadian Pacific's Pacific liners hosted many illustrious names. The great Chinese nationalist leaders Dr. Sun Yat-sen and Chiang Kai-Shek travelled between Hong Kong and Shanghai on board the *Empress of Russia*. Dr. Sun Yat-sen also used Canadian Pacific's vessels on several of his voyages to and from North America. Celebrities such as Babe Ruth and other professional American baseball players, including Lou Gehrig, undertook a twenty-two-game barnstorming tour of the Far East in 1934, travelling with CP. They were met by the adulation of enormous crowds in Japan, where baseball was very popular.

There were royal passengers, too. In 1931, King Prajadhipok of Siam (now Thailand) travelled on the *Empress of Japan* for eye surgery in the United States. After an extended visit in both Canada and the US, the King and his wife returned home in October of that year. In 1937, the younger brother of Emperor Hirohito, Prince Chichibu, and his wife spent eleven days in Canada on their way to London for the coronation of King George VI, including a visit to Canadian Pacific's Hotel Vancouver.

After their crossing of the Pacific, the first stop for the Canadian Pacific *Empresses* was Yokohama, Japan, located 29 kilometres (17 miles) south of Tokyo. As the major port of entry for Japan, Yokohama, with its shops, hotels, and modern facilities, was a major tourist centre. One can only imagine the passengers' excitement at this first contact with the Orient.

Canadian Pacific's vessels then headed from Japan to China and the treaty port of Shanghai. This was a major port of call for Western travellers to the Orient and a significant attraction among Canadian Pacific's travel options. The town's location at the mouth of the Yangtze River, roughly equidistant from Peking (Beijing) and Hong Kong made it the premier centre of commerce for the whole China coast.

In spite of the turbulence of this period in China's history, the city's commercial and cultural world flourished, with over one hundred thousand foreigners and refugees living within it borders. The Shanghai of the interwar period was a profoundly interesting port of call, world famous for its colourful lifestyle.

The bund, or embankment, along the Huangpu River was the centre of Shanghai's commerce, with numerous internationally owned banks, trading companies, and foreign consulates along its main street. Located north of the old walled city of Shanghai, British and American settlements were combined into

Left: The "All Red" British Empire line at work: Sir Cecil Clementi, KCMG, governor of Hong Kong from 1925 to 1930, arriving in the colony on board Canadian Pacific's *Empress of Russia*, May 27, 1928.

Facing page, top: Babe Ruth departing for Japan on board the *Empress of Japan*, October 20, 1934

Facing page, bottom left: The King and Queen of Siam (Thailand) leaving Canadian Pacific's *Empress of Japan* in Vancouver, April 16, 1931

Facing page, bottom right: Crown Prince and Princess Chichibu of the Japanese royal family on the rooftop tea garden of Canadian Pacific's second Hotel Vancouver, March 29, 1937

the International Settlement, and just to the south of it was the equally large French Bund, part of the French Concession. These settlements were renowned for their fine architecture, and as part of the treaty port, both of these foreign areas were outside Chinese national control.

During the interwar period, tens of thousands of Chinese flocked to Shanghai to profit from its commercial opportunities and the relative security and freedom it offered. The nightlife in the city during this period was notorious, and Shanghai's large publishing industry allowed for a flourishing of the graphic arts that captured the beauty and romance of this flamboyant period. Offering service to this thriving city contributed to Canadian Pacific's cosmopolitan image.

During the early twentieth century, Hong Kong remained the Asian hub for Canadian Pacific's fleets. Benefiting from its British-run commerce and the security of its strategic location, Canadian Pacific could organize its routes and shipping to deal with local traffic and at the same time refit its vessels at the Kowloon dockyards, located on the mainland, across from Hong Kong Island. With its busy harbour, attractive colonial architecture, and colourful mix of populations, all set against the beauty of its mountainous backdrop, Hong Kong was always one of the most popular ports of call for the passengers of the company's regular liners and cruise ships.

Jastest to the ORIENT

The White Empresses of the Pacific

CANADIAN PACIFIC

Top: Yokohama street scene, c. 1908. This stereoscopic photo would have been sold as a tourist souvenir.

Bottom: Canadian Pacific poster, c. 1930

Facing page, top: Aerial view of Hong Kong with the Kowloon dockyards across the harbour, c. 1930

Facing page, bottom: The French Bund in Shanghai, c. 1931

View from the peak. H.K.

SEE THIS WORLD BEFORE THE NEXT

The notion of the holiday cruise began to emerge in the early nineteenth century, soon after the invention of the steamboat, but it was only in 1900 that the first purpose-built cruise ship was constructed. With the rise of the middle class during the boom of the Roaring Twenties, the cruising market greatly expanded and the industry took off. Canadian Pacific decided in 1924 that the next stage in its growth would be its expansion into the cruising business on a regular basis. Many of its passenger liners were tied up during the winter months and could be used on cruises in Caribbean and Mediterranean waters. All told, the company offered over five hundred cruises during its history, and fittingly for the world's "Greatest Travel System," its excursions crossed all seven oceans of the world and touched the shores of all of its continents.

It is also important to note that from 1915 onwards, Canadian Pacific's ocean shipping operations were separated from its Canadian rail operations and based first in Liverpool and then, from 1921 onwards, in Southampton. The vast majority of its crews were of British origin, and of the cruises offered by the company, almost half emanated from the UK, hosting a large number of British passengers.

Quality shore excursions and ground transportation were a trademark of Canadian Pacific's cruise operations and were facilitated by its international network of shipping agents and sales operations.

THE WEST INDIES

The West Indies was a popular winter cruising destination for both Canadian Pacific's North American and British travellers. Its excursions ranged in length from five days to a month and included not only the islands of the Eastern and Western Caribbean but also mainland ports in Panama, Colombia, and Venezuela.

THE MEDITERRANEAN

———

Top: Canadian Pacific West Indies cruise poster, 1937

Bottom: Canadian Pacific West Indies cruise poster, 1936

Facing pages: Canadian Pacific cruise passengers at the Sphinx

Preceding pages: Passengers disembark from the *Empress of Scotland* at Naples, c. 1928

Pages 126-127: Canadian Pacific world cruise poster, 1923

By far the most popular of Canadian Pacific's cruises were the twenty-two day itineraries that the company ran each year in the Mediterranean. Travellers, then as now, went to the birthplace of Western civilization to discover their cultural roots and their heritage, visiting sites made famous to them since the earliest days of their childhood.

Mediterranean cruises leaving from New York City started with a seven-day crossing and could run up to two and a half months in duration. Popular stops along the way included Madeira, Cadiz, Algiers, and Majorca, before visiting ports in southern and northern Italy. From Dubrovnik on the east coast of the Adriatic, the ships sailed to Athens and through the Greek Isles of the Aegean Sea and the Straits of the Dardanelles to reach the Bosphorus and fabled Constantinople (Istanbul).

Next was the Holy Land. After landing at the Palestinian port of Haifa, in the Bay of Acre, a train took passengers on to Jerusalem. Unfortunately, the port of Haifa had become clogged with silt in the interwar period, and large vessels could not dock there. Instead, passengers were obliged to tender ashore by barge, after first being lowered in a large, enclosed wicker basket from the moving deck of the ship, high above. It was an unforgettable experience for all involved.

After several days in Jerusalem, most passengers travelled by train to Cairo to explore the city and partake in visits of the nearby Giza Pyramids and Sphinx. Optional excursions to Luxor, Karnak, Thebes, and the Valley of the Kings were also available.

At the end of their five-day visit in Egypt, cruise passengers travelled to Port Said to join their ship at the northern end of the Suez Canal. This was followed by another brief stop in Italy and a visit to Monaco, before the cruise ended in Cherbourg or Southampton.

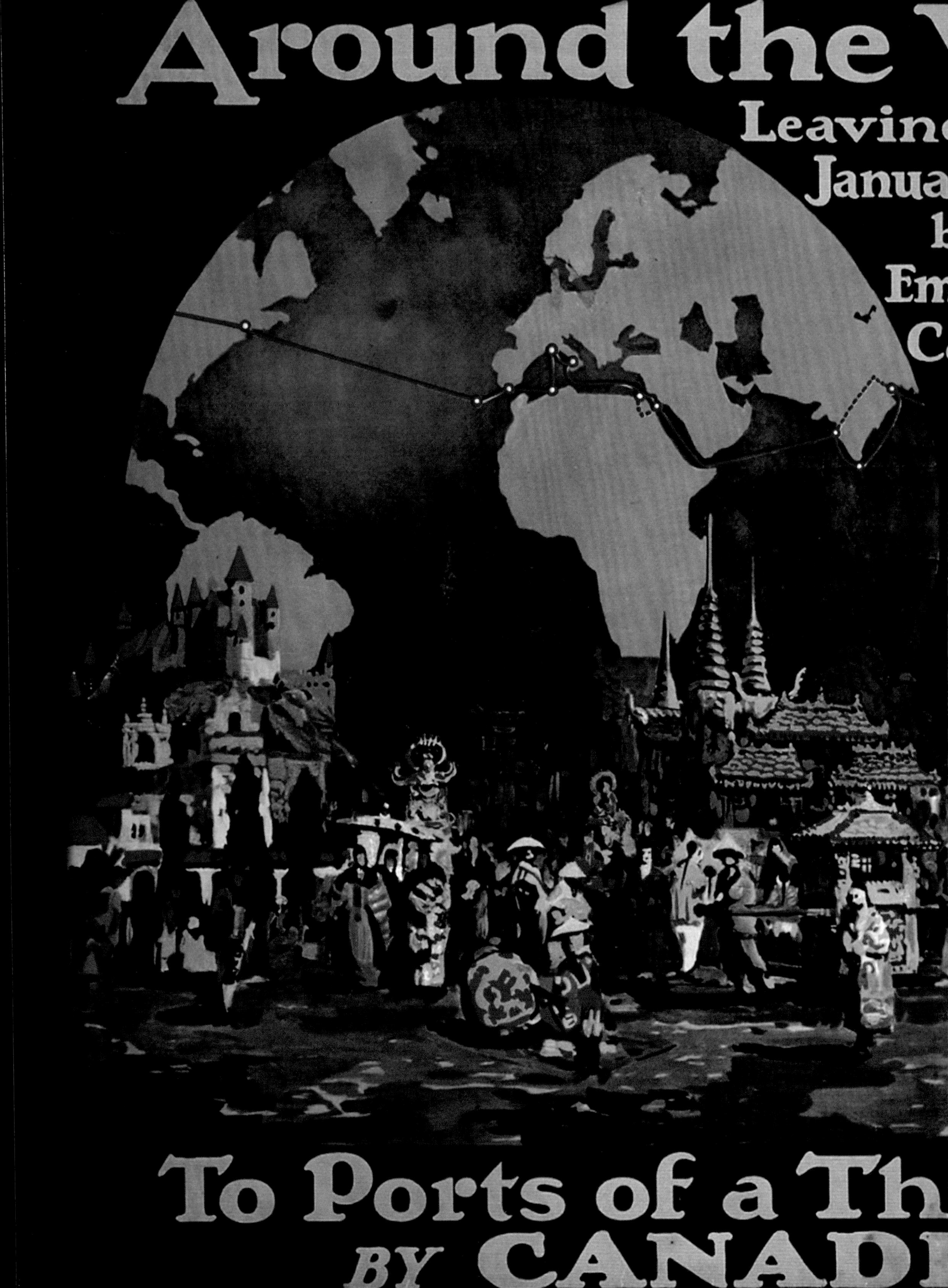
Around the
Leavin
Janua
Em
To Ports of a Th
BY CANAD

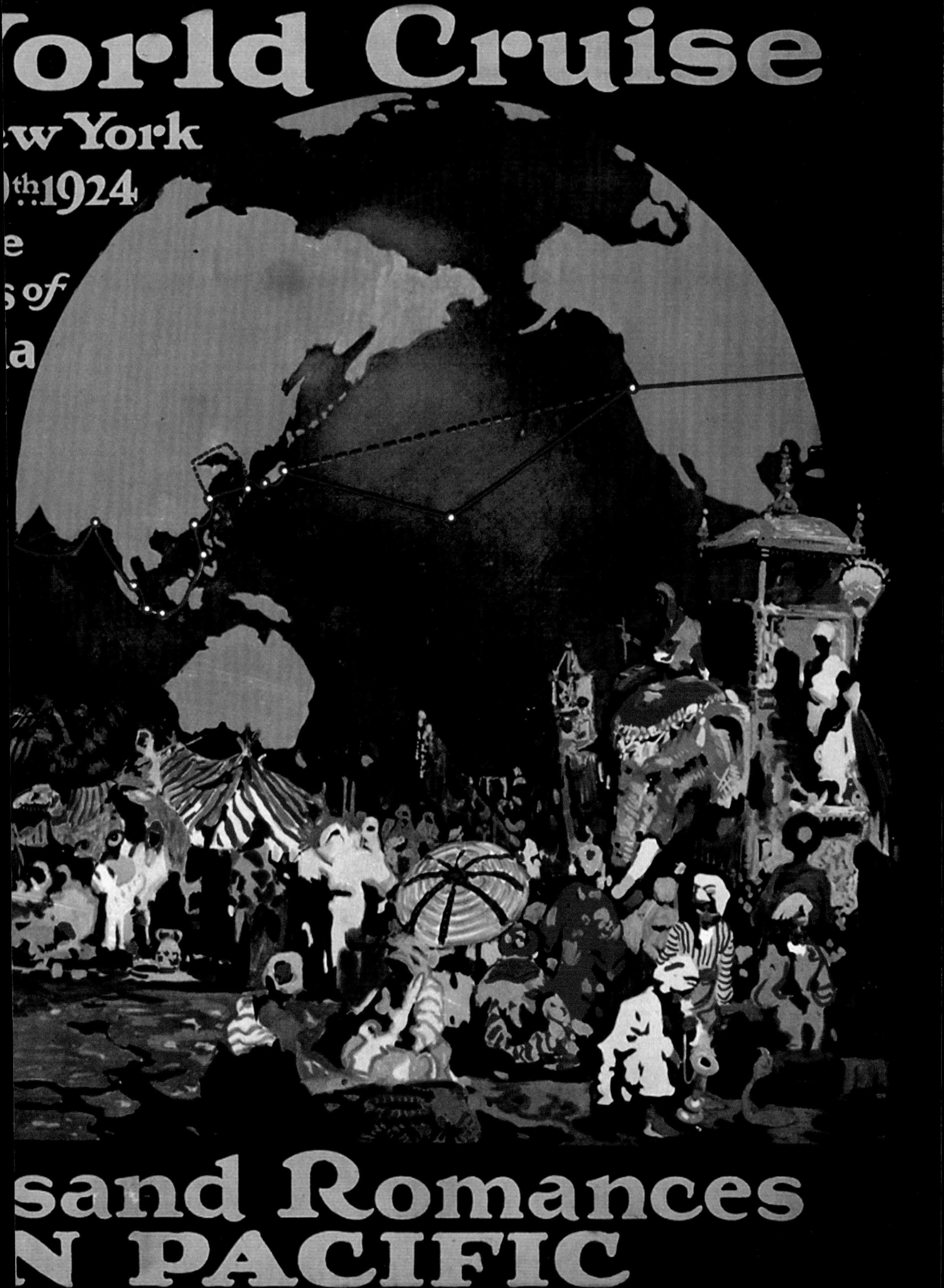
orld Cruise
ew York
th 1924
e
s of
a
sand Romances
N PACIFIC

WORLD CRUISES

Each year, one of the company's larger vessels was used on a luxury four-month, round-the-world trip. The circumnavigation started in December or January in New York City—and crossed the Atlantic—or in Southampton, then on to the Mediterranean and to the Holy Land. From the Suez Canal, the ships travelled through the Red Sea and Indian Ocean to Bombay (Mumbai). Passengers then had the option to disembark the ship and cross the subcontinent by rail, normally joining the vessel in Ceylon (Sri Lanka). From Ceylon, the ships continued to the Far East, reaching China and Japan before crossing the Pacific and returning to New York and Southampton via the Panama Canal. Between 1923 and 1939, the company undertook a total of seventeen such circumnavigations.

Canadian Pacific had a wonderful marketing theme for its world cruises. They were publicized as a four-month excursion into spring, in which one was continually celebrating the arrival of the season in the areas that the ship was visiting. In actual fact, many of the photos taken in the more northerly latitudes of these circumnavigations show the passengers in heavy winter coats, huddling against the cold. Even more provocative was the company adage for these cruises: "See This World Before The Next!"

Arriving in the Mediterranean, more passengers joined the cruise, most of them hailing from the United Kingdom.

CP's *Empress of Australia* in New York Harbor, c. 1922

The resulting mix of old world and new world passengers was fascinating and at times included well-known American heiresses, British aristocracy, and Indian royalty. To emphasize this elite presence, a copy of *Burke's Peerage* was laid out in the ship's library, next to that of an American *Who's Who*. In truth, however, the most of the passengers were members of their respective middle classes—retired school teachers, etc.—for whom this voyage represented the dream of a lifetime. And mix they did, for most of Canadian Pacific's world cruises registered all of its passengers as first class.

After completing the initial legs of a Mediterranean itinerary, world cruises were organized to arrive in the Holy Land during the Christmas period to celebrate this important religious event at the scene of Christ's birth. Touring in Egypt followed and then the passengers travelled south by rail to Suez, at the southern end of the Suez Canal, and joined their ship at the entrance to the Red Sea.

INDIA AND THE FAR EAST

As the ship sailed to Bombay for the next eight days through the Red Sea and the Indian Ocean, the weather grew hot, and the excitement of the passengers increased. They were finally heading East!

M.F. Bridie, passenger on the first world cruise of the RMS *Empress of Britain* in 1931–32 described her elation in her published diary, *Round the World Without a Pinprick*.

We are really on our way East now. Everything is quite tropical-looking now. People are all out and about in light summery garb, which is so much more charming than heavy tweeds on board ship. The officers all in white duck look quite irresistible. [Their cap peaks were decorated with maple leaves to represent Canada.] Bellhops run about in white too, with orange pipings and white caps shaped like a glengarry. The velvet chairs in the dining-room have now their cool blue glazed linen covers.

Today has been perfectly perfect again, wonderful sunshine, skies as blue, deep strong cloudless blue, as they could possibly be. There is a real zephyr blowing; we are never fearfully hot; one does not stay in the sun for any long period.

I feel so well, so fresh, so very young and energetic, in fact, so physically magnificent, I just enjoy every minute.

Above: Canadian Pacific Mediterranean brochure, 1931

Facing page: CP poster, c. 1936. Printed for the government of India.

The Taj Mahal

LIFE ON BOARD

Life on board these long cruises was surprisingly occupied. The ships normally travelled by night so that the passengers could go ashore for excursions during the day. But of course on such a long itinerary there were many days at sea where one experienced what was called "normal life." This life consisted of three formal meals a day plus four o'clock tea, interspersed with the "daily dozen," about four miles of walking around the decks, refreshing laps in the swimming pool, and numerous sporting competitions of tennis, cricket, squash, and deck games.

One also had to spend time in one's deck chair to take the sun and breeze and socialize with new-found friends among the hundreds of other passengers on board. During this period, letter writing and diary keeping were also important pastimes so the pleasure of the trip could be shared with family and friends. In the larger ports, mail was regularly received and sent, and mail call on board was a major point of excitement for all the passengers.

In the evening there were almost always scheduled activities, which varied from shore lectures, musical recitals, quizzes, and games to fancy dress evenings and variety nights put on by the passengers themselves. Once the organized events were over, the passengers danced, finishing their evening well after midnight with a refreshing dip in the ship's pool. It was a demanding schedule, as they often had to be up again by seven to have breakfast before heading off on shore excursions, but at the same time it was great and exhilarating fun, both for them and the crews that served them, as M.F. Bridie recorded.

Last night we had an extraordinarily good circus. It included real clowns, who ran and tumbled about, getting into all sorts of spontaneous mischief. Trained elephants and dancing bears, snake-charmers, etc., etc. There was a bullfight, an exhibition of freaks... the Strong Man was quite the best. He was Mr. Illum from Copenhagen, a stout, elderly man, with a beaming smile like Mr. Pickwick. He just lived the part, so much so that it was quite a shock when his weights were whisked away by the littlest bell-hops.

And on Sundays, the divine service was undertaken:

The Prayer Books provided are the nice big size, bound in leather, and are stamped in gold letters, "Canadian Pacific Railway." A small table is covered with the Union Jack and on this is the enormous Prayer Book and Bible. A number of the ship's crew and officers, all in spotless white duck, file in looking a little self-conscious. A dozen little messenger boys, also in pure white and a few young office girls, form the choir.... There are usually about 130, all told, mostly English people, and the rest American. There is something curiously traditional about the serious way the English of this social class take church. The Earl and Countess always turn up. The army and navy are fully represented. The Lieut-Colonel, the handsomest man on board, stands to attention at the singing and rolls out the responses with the usual determination to do his duty... then we pray for our beloved King, the President of the United States, and the rulers and governors of other countries, and then for our Royal family."

After eight days of sailing, the world cruise passengers arrived at Bombay, India, to visit the "Jewel in the Crown"

———

Below, left to right:

HRH the Duke of Kent (left) on board CP's *Duchess of Richmond* in the West Indies, 1935. The fourth son of George V, the duke was thirty-three in 1935 and very much a member of the "fast set" of London social life. He married in November 1934; perhaps this voyage marked a belated honeymoon trip.

Passengers on the first day of a cruise lunch with the captain, on board CP's *Empress of France*, sailing from New York, c. 1920s. The *Empress of France* was used for the first three of the company's world cruises. A number of single women are sitting at the table. Many upper- and middle-class women of this period were adventuresome travellers and often chose cruises for the personal security and facilities that the ships provided.

Group of Canadian Pacific cruise passengers in front of the Taj Mahal at Agra, c. 1930

of the British Empire. Most of the passengers then left the ship and travelled across the subcontinent on specially organized trains to see Delhi, Agra, Benares, Calcutta, and Darjeeling. These trains then returned to the ship at Bombay or headed south to the temple town of Madurai and the east coast port of Madras, where the passengers were ferried over to the island of Ceylon to join their ship at Colombo.

From Ceylon the cruise headed into the Far East through the Strait of Malacca. After visiting the Straits Settlements of Penang, some passengers travelled by rail and private car for an 800-kilometre (500-mile) journey across Malaysia and Siam to reach the ruins of Angkor Wat in Cambodia. Others continued with the vessel to visit the islands of Sumatra, Java, and Bali in the Dutch East Indies before heading to the tip of the peninsula to visit the British colony of Singapore.

SINGAPORE

Singapore has been a well-known name from my earliest years, and it was with real excitement that I first approached the beautiful bay.... A young sailor swings a small coloured bundle of bunting to the head of each mast. A bell rings; the flag is broken, and we see the red and white squares of the C.P.R. house flag on the forward mast, and the flag of the country we are approaching on the aft mast. An enormous Union Jack hangs from the stern when we are in harbour. Good Lord! How we love it!

Majestically we move toward the quay. It is easy to see which is ours, for the crowds are already lining all the points of vantage. All along the rails our passengers are gazing out, cameras and ciné-Kodaks are busy. [This was the first docking of the *Empress of Britain* in Singapore, probably the largest and most luxurious vessel the colony had ever seen.]

Nearer yet the waiting crowd becomes individualized. Oh, the colour, the kaleidoscope of these Eastern ports. Is there any sight in the world more penetrating, more memorable, and indeed more significant? Every shade and every shape can be seen, dark skins against dazzling white, bright blue trousers, shirts of many colours.

The spotless topees of the Europeans are as noticeable as their strong decided faces; these are the pioneers who have forsaken many of the comforts of Old England for the more adventurous life of the East. Jews and Parthians, Cretes and Arabians, and farther round Japanese and Chinese, Siamese and Maoris, negroes and Filipinos, men of every nation, every creed, and every race seem to foregather on a foreign quay to greet an arrival from the other side of the world."

—M.F. Bridie, World Cruise, *Empress of Britain* 1931–32

After Singapore, the cruise continued up through the Gulf of Thailand to Bangkok, and the ship steamed an enormous distance of 2,600 kilometres (1,430 nautical miles) across the South China Sea to Manila, the capital of the Philippines. Throughout this part of the voyage, the weather remained stifling hot.

HONG KONG

The vessel then headed north to the China coast for a four-day stay at Canadian Pacific's base at Hong Kong. Here, the cruise ships would often meet other Canadian Pacific vessels on their regular runs from Canada. Hong Kong was always a favourite stop for the passengers, who found everything exotic and beautiful and the shopping fantastic. M.F. Bridie wrote in her diary:

It was really a wonderful sail up the harbour [Hong Kong] at sunrise. The straits run for several miles between high hills without much vegetation, but showing reddish soil and the granite rocks.... The form and colouring of the hills are simply exquisite. The sun rose as we steamed in and tipped the mountain peaks with gold and pink. On every side of us were boats of every description, size and nationality—a number of British gunboats and cruisers....

The island of Hong Kong appears [from the harbour] to be just one enormous mountain with the city of Victoria all round its base and villas dotted all over its sides. It reminds one of Naples, but seems closer together, and the harbour is smaller. At night it is a particularly lovely sight. Brilliant lights surround the foot like a black velvet ornament richly studded with diamonds. Higher up the lights are more scattered, then near the top is a curiously realistic arrangement of lights called the "dragon."

All the shop signs or names are printed perpendicularly in Chinese fashion on the pillars of the colonnades, frequently in bright colours while long coloured banners also hang out to catch the eye of shoppers. This always gives a festive appearance as if the street were decorated; moreover, on the balconies above, clothes of all colours, hung out to dry, accentuate this impression. There are thousands of rickshas everywhere, and sedan chairs too....

Hong Kong is indeed a shopper's paradise.... I bought rich silk nightdresses, beautifully embroidered.... There was carved ivory and jade, embroidered silk shawls and kimonos that just make one's mouth water, beautiful carved camphor wood chests, and carved chairs. The vendors clustered round the boat, bringing peacock chairs, cane hampers and baskets. It is great fun bargaining with these people, and it needs an astute buyer to know the real value of the goods.

Flowers are wonderfully cheap, and we got great bunches of glorious exotic blooms and graceful baskets of exquisite colours.... A good many of us brought baskets on board with us and the dining room looks a perfect bower of bright colours.

The boat is also filled with the singing of canaries and the chirping of daintily-coloured love birds. Many of the passengers brought them on board....

CHINA

Leaving Hong Kong, the cruise continued to Shanghai and then further north to Chinwangtao, a port that offered a railway journey of 291 kilometres (180 miles) to Peking to view the capital and its Forbidden City. From Peking, one could take a five-hour trip by a special train to the Great Wall, another of the major highlights of the cruise.

The presence on trains of warlord soldiers who acted as guards for the passengers reflected the turbulence and turmoil of China in this period, when civil war raged through much of the country. The danger of violence escalated with

The Great Wall at Peking. *Empress of Australia* world cruise, 1927–28

the increasing incursions of Japan into the country. During its 1938 world cruise, Canadian Pacific cancelled its scheduled stops in mainland China and headed south from Hong Kong towards Australia and the islands of New Zealand.

JAPAN

Next was Japan, with a stop at Kobe and a two-day train trip to Kyoto, the historic capital of the Shoguns, and Nara, another former capital, famous for Nara Park and its sacred deer. The final port of call was Yokohama and the nearby capital of Tokyo. After the relative chaos and disarray of China, the serenity and order of Japan always elicited a strong reaction from the passengers.

In 1926, for the first time, Canadian Pacific also included the small Japanese resort town of Beppu. Famous for its mineral baths and more than three hundred inns and hotels, the arrival of Canadian Pacific's enormous cruise ships caused a sensation in the town and incited a tremendous welcome from its citizens.

HOT WEATHER!

In contrast with the cold weather experienced in the Mediterranean during the earlier part of the cruise, the temperature on board was now stifling hot, and most sightseeing was relegated "to the freshness of the morning hours." The intense heat continued for some six weeks until the vessel turned north to Hong Kong and the China coast. Such extremes of hot and cold were one of the realities of travel in the golden age.

> Ever since we left Ceylon there has been a strong wind and a heavy sea in the Indian Ocean, which lasted for two days. We crossed the Equator at 7 p.m. on Sunday night and the heat was simply intolerable, very heavy and muggy, no sun but wet steam everywhere. Temperature in dining room was 96 degrees and in my stateroom 93 degrees in the middle of the night. The perspiration simply ran off us in rivulets. I have never imagined it could be so hot anywhere.
> —M.F. Bridie, World Cruise, *Empress of Britain* 1931–32

THE MOST BEAUTIFUL

At the end of the 1931–32 world cruise, passengers were asked to vote for the most beautiful places they had seen their journey. M.F. Bridie recorded the winning names:

> The most beautiful city, Honolulu.
> The most beautiful country, Japan.
> The most beautiful edifice, Taj Mahal.
> The most beautiful harbour, Hong-kong.
> The most beautiful island, Oahu
>   (Hawaiian Isles).
> The most beautiful ladies, Japanese.
> The most beautiful mountain, Fujisan.
> The most beautiful stream, Nile.
> The most beautiful view, from Peak,
>   Hong-kong.

The overwhelming dominance of the Far East in this list undoubtedly reflected the extremely cold weather the cruise had experienced in the Mediterranean, but it also speaks to the exotic appeal of the Orient in the mind of the Western traveller — an appeal that Canadian Pacific was uniquely positioned to service.

Clockwise from left:

Miss Katherine Kinney of Albany, New York, with friends in kimonos, 1926. Miss Kinney (centre), the daughter of an Albany attorney, travelled with her aunt on the *Empress of Scotland*'s world tour of 1925–26. Her travels were reported in the Albany newspaper. It was the voyage of a lifetime for her.

Miss Katherine Kinney, "On the lap of the Gods." The Lotus Buddha, Kamakura, Japan, 1926.

Guards on special train to Peking. *Empress of Australia* world cruise, 1927–28.

Beppu, reception of cruise passengers, 1928. *Empress of Australia* world cruise, 1927–28.

Children of Kyoto receiving American friendship dolls from the tour group. *Empress of Australia* world cruise, 1927–28.

Overleaf: The *Empress of Britain* docking in Woolloomooloo Bay (Sydney), Australia, April 2, 1938

THE WORLD'S WONDER SHIP

The success of its cruises and regular passenger liners encouraged Canadian Pacific in 1930 to launch a remarkable new ship, the second named the *Empress of Britain*. With a length of 231 metres (758 feet) and 42,348 gross registered tons, the vessel was by far the largest ship ever to have been involved in the "Canada Trade," and its service speed of twenty-four knots allowed it to shorten the time of an Atlantic crossing to Canada to just under five days.

Called the "Five Day Atlantic Giantess," "Canada's Challenger," and the "The World's Wonder Ship," the *Empress of Britain* was one of Canadian Pacific's greatest achievements. Although not as big or as fast as the major liners on the Atlantic run to New York, such as the *Queen Mary* or the *Normandie*, the ship's fine lines, glistening white hull, and powerful buff funnels made it one of the most beautiful and recognizable liners of the era.

The *Empress of Britain* was one of the first liners ever designed to also serve as a cruise ship on a regular basis. With its luxurious fittings and spaciousness, it successfully hosted the world's elite for as much as four months at a time. During the summer months it operated as a liner between Europe and Canada with a capacity of almost 1,200 passengers. In the winter months it undertook the company's famous round-the-world cruise, carrying anywhere from 300 to 700 first-class passengers. The crew of over 700 men and women offered one of the highest crew-to-passenger ratios of any large vessel.

On June 1, 1931, the *Empress of Britain* arrived for the first time in Quebec. The vessel's masts were too high for it to travel further upstream and pass under the Jacques Cartier Bridge to enter the port of Montreal, and so its home port was Quebec City, where it docked at a passenger terminal especially constructed for the new ship.

To facilitate rail connections further inland from Quebec, a mile-long tunnel was constructed under the rock of the city to link the new terminal to the existing rail lines.

A crowd of over one hundred thousand watched the vessel during its first approach to Quebec City and its docking at the Anse au Foulon, below the Plains of Abraham. The film idols Douglas Fairbanks and Mary Pickford were on board. Several days later a gala dinner was given on board that included Prime Minister R.B. Bennett and many other Canadian dignitaries.

The vessel's fine interior decoration very much emphasized its Canadian origins. A mural depicting the arrival of Hélène Boullé at Quebec City in 1620 decorated the landing of the ship's lounge deck. The wife of Samuel de Champlain, the founder of Quebec, Hélène Boullé was one of the first European women to come to Canada.

The Mayfair Lounge was the *Empress of Britain*'s finest public room. The lounge's classical design, with jade green columns and a frieze bordering the ceiling, was typical of the conservative style that still dominated many passenger vessels of this period. Its "classical" frieze, however, was decorated with Canadian elements such as maple leaves, snowshoes, and beavers!

———

Empress of Britain, new Atlantic Giantess, Canadian Pacific travel brochure: "Introducing a new era in World Cruising … offering unparalleled size, speed and super-luxuriousness. 42,500 Tons Gross Register, 63,750 Tons Displacement, 758 Feet Long."

CANADIAN PACIFIC

EMPRESS OF BRITAIN

KENNETH D
SHOESMITH

TO CANADA & USA

Of totally different design was the ship's Cathay Lounge, created to emphasize the company's link with the Pacific and the Far East. And the *Empress*'s sports deck alone was over 139 metres (455 feet) long, more spacious than on any other ship afloat, and the first-ever regulation-size tennis court on board a passenger vessel was located behind the ship's funnels.

From 1931 through 1939, the *Empress of Britain* undertook eight world cruises for the company. Each of these cruises involved as much as 55,500 kilometres (30,000 nautical miles) of travel and stops in as many as eighty-one ports in twenty-three countries. The *Empress of Britain* was the largest and most luxurious ship at that time to have ever sailed through both the Suez and Panama Canals.

During the economically depressed 1930s, the ship carried an average of approximately three hundred passengers, less than half of the seven hundred that it could accommodate on these cruises. All the world-cruise passengers were considered first class, and the price of a cabin started at $1,600.

Above: The lounge deck landing of the *Empress of Britain* with mural of Hélène Boullé in background

Left: Dancing in the Mayfair Lounge, *Empress of Britain*, 1931

Facing page: *Empress of Britain*, Canadian Pacific poster, 1933

Overleaf: The Mayfair Lounge, *Empress of Britain*

The top two suites on board, however, cost over $12,000. To put this in perspective, the average annual salary for a Canadian family during the Depression years was $1,200.

The Sino-Japanese War suddenly altered the *Empress of Britain*'s 1938 world-cruise itinerary. After the regular visit to Hong Kong, the ship went south to Australia and New Zealand. That year, Australia was celebrating the 150th anniversary of the arrival of its first European settlers, with events planned throughout the country. As a Canadian vessel, the *Empress* was a veritable symbol of the might of the British Empire and its far-reaching dominions, which helped add pride to the historical festivities.

Above: The *Empress of Britain*'s full-sized tennis court

Facing page: The *Empress of Britain* passing under San Francisco's Golden Gate Bridge on its 1931–32 world cruise. At the time, it was the largest vessel to have ever sailed in Californian waters and attracted enormous attention.

On April 2, 1938, the *Empress of Britain* approached the entrance to Sydney Harbour as over thirty thousand people lined the approaches to view the largest vessel to have ever sailed in Antipodean waters. Ultimately, because of the height of its masts, the ship could not pass under the Sydney Harbour Bridge and had to dock in nearby Woolloomooloo Bay.

From Sydney, many of the *Empress*'s passengers travelled by rail to Melbourne, where they joined the ship before it sailed for New Zealand's capital of Wellington on the South Island. The ship spent one day docked at Wellington and drew thousands of spectators. Another four days were spent in Auckland, on the North Island, where tens of thousands of New Zealanders came to wonder at the size and beauty of the Canadian vessel.

Shore excursions in New Zealand included a visit to Rotorua and its famous Whakarewarewa Thermal Valley, 225 kilometres (140 miles) southeast of Auckland. Lying in a lake district, the town is situated on a caldera known for its geothermal activity and geysers.

Rotorua was once the site of the Maori fortress of Te Puia, first occupied around 1325, and known to the Maori

as an impenetrable stronghold never taken in battle. Maori have lived there ever since, taking full advantage of the geothermal activity in the valley for heating and cooking. It is an area of sacred significance to them.

Above: Rice Fields in Bali, *Empress of Britain* world cruise, c. 1930s

Facing page: Thermal Village in Rotorua, New Zealand. A Maori woman feeds a Maori Tohunga, a priest who is under *tapu*, spiritual restriction. The English word *taboo* derives from this word. *Empress of Britain* world cruise, 1931–32.

Overleaf: National Australian Travel Association poster, c. 1930s

Overleaf, facing page: New Zealand Department of Tourist and Health Resorts poster, c.1930s

ROYAL VISITS

Throughout the nineteenth century, members of the British royal family had made occasional visits to Canada, most as part of active military service. But not since 1860, when the Prince of Wales formally visited both Canada and the United States, had there been a true royal visit with all its pageantry and ceremony. As such, the visit in 1901 of the Duke and Duchess of Cornwall and York—the Duke soon to become Prince of Wales and direct heir to the British throne—caused a tremendous rush of excitement in Canada.

This excitement, for most Canadians, was heightened by the knowledge that they were part of the "Greatest Empire The World Had Ever Known." The growing insecurity of the era, with Britain's ongoing Boer War and the rising threat of a powerful and militant Germany, accentuated these emotions. Imperial passions were running at a level never seen before, and the royal visit was, in fact, part of an exhausting round-the-world tour of all the dominions—India, Australia, New Zealand, and Canada—designed to focus citizens' attention on the future needs of the empire.

For Canada and Canadian Pacific, the visit marked an extraordinary opportunity to show their loyalty and usefulness to the British Crown. Without the railway it would have been impossible for the Duke and Duchess to create the pageantry and visibility that they wished to achieve. Canadian Pacific provided a special nine-car train for the royal party of twenty-two people, which the British press described as a "palace on wheels, and a marvel to all who beheld it."

Ultimately, the company's contribution to the royal visit, and to royal trips in 1919, 1924, 1927, and 1939, represented the fulfillment of the early dream of George Stephen, the founder of the line, to link Canada to the

rest of the British Empire, with an "All Red Line" to the Orient. This was the web of empire or, as Canadian Pacific modestly described itself, "The Empire's Greatest Railway."

AN IMPERIAL DESCENT WORTHY OF THE EMPIRE

Sir Donald Mackenzie Wallace, KCIE, KCVO, assistant private secretary to the Duke of Cornwall, described the descent of the Kicking Horse Pass and its canyon as follows, putting the experience in an imperial perspective:

> Nothing indeed could be grander than the views
> as we descend from the Great Divide to the broad
> valley of the Columbia through the famous gorges of
> the Kicking Horse River, a boisterous torrent which

Above: The Duke and Duchess en route to Vancouver, September 30, 1901, on board the Canadian Pacific "royal train," at Field, BC, after passing through the Kicking Horse Pass. For their return journey up the pass, five Canadian Pacific locomotives pulled the nine-car train.

Facing page: North West Mounted Police parade with the royal party at Calgary. The Duke, in a bearskin hat, centre left, rides with them. The Duke and Duchess noted that many of the riders wore decorations for their recent service for the empire in the Boer War, September 28, 1901.

Preceding pages: The Prince of Wales, inaugurating Union Station in Toronto, August 6, 1927

rushes downwards by leaps and bounds. In size the mountains cannot pretend to rival those seen from Darjiling and other points in the Himalaya, but one gets much nearer to them. From Darjiling one sees the hoary Kinchinjunga miles and miles away, whereas here we pass so near some of the highest mountains that it looks as if from the summit one might throw a pebble on to the roof of the cars. The railway is constructed along the rocky banks of the torrent, and right and left rise precipices to a height of several thousand feet. On the left the mountains may be almost said to overhang the line, so that we have to leave our staterooms and stand on the platform between the cars in order to see the summits!

It can be difficult today to comprehend the strength of the imperial connection in the Canada of over a century ago. Canadians saw themselves as living in the senior dominion of the most powerful empire on the planet, and the visit of a future king had something incredibly exotic and magical about it. Thanks to Canadian Pacific and its royal train, Canadians had the chance to see their future monarch and his consort in the flesh. The *Daily Colonist*, a Victoria newspaper, summed up the general sentiment:

> The Royal reception is over. The echoes of the cheers have died away. The lights, which made the city a fairyland, have been extinguished. And what remains? Not simply loyalty to the Motherland, our King,

Clockwise from above:

The Duke and Dutchess of York and Cornwall, the future King George V and Queen Mary, 1901

The royal train travelling through the lower canyon of the Kicking Horse River, September 30, 1901

The *Empress of India* with the Duke and Duchess disembarking at Victoria on Vancouver Island, October 1, 1901

The royal couple pass by the CPR Vancouver station as they continue into the city for a parade and royal reception, September 31, 1901

Vancouver, September 31, 1901, with assembled sailors and dignitaries, as the Duke and Duchess embark in their carriage for a procession through the city. The royal train is behind them and the *Empress of India* at the dock, waiting to take them to Vancouver Island the following day.

and our institutions, for this we always felt to such a degree that it could not be intensified. Not simply a sense of the greatness and unity of the Empire, for this we have always realised, and we have cemented the bond of union with the blood of our best manhood. [The ongoing Boer War would ultimately see the deaths of 276 of the 7,000 Canadians who served in the conflict.] Something else remains, and it is something new—something that the people have never felt before. It is a feeling of personal affection and esteem for the Heir-Apparent and the gracious lady whose life, happiness, and future are so closely bound up with his.

EDWARD, PRINCE OF WALES: 1919 AND 1927

Edward, Prince of Wales, the eldest son of King George V and Queen Mary, visited Canada officially on three different occasions, in 1919, 1924, and 1927, and made several other unofficial visits to his E.P. Ranch, which he bought in 1919, in the foothills of southern Alberta. On all three official visits, Canadian Pacific trains and personnel played an instrumental role in the success of the tours.

As heir to the throne, Edward often represented his father, George V, at home and abroad. From 1919 through to 1935 he undertook sixteen tours of the empire and was met with tremendous enthusiasm wherever he went. His rank, sophistication, charm, good looks, and unmarried status made him the most photographed celebrity of his time.

Top: The Duke and Duchess of York and Cornwall visiting Banff, Alberta, on October 4, 1901, with an escort of North West Mounted Police. They later dined at Canadian Pacific's Banff Springs Hotel.

Centre: The Prince of Wales inspecting the Canadian Highland Regiment in Vancouver, September 1919

Bottom: Edward, Prince of Wales (left), and his brother Prince George at the Canadian Pacific railway station in Vancouver, August 18, 1927

Facing page: Their Royal Highnesses returning east via the Fraser Valley, October 3, 1901, more or less on board the royal train. Enjoying a hot ride on a cowcatcher at a sizzling twenty miles an hour through the mountains.

In late August of 1919, the twenty-five-year-old Edward arrived in Canada on board a British warship and boarded a beautiful nine-car royal train provided by Canadian Pacific. The locomotive of the train flew two special flags and had the Royal Coat of Arms emblazoned on its side. The rear carriage that was provided for the Prince's personal use was the Kilarney, the private rail car of Lord Shaughnessy, the president of the line. Its sides were also emblazoned in gold with the royal motto. An observation platform offered wonderful vistas of the country and allowed the Prince to give impromtu speeches to the thousands of loyal Canadians who gathered to see him at every stop.

The Prince undertook an unprecedented two-month rail tour of the country that included a visit to Ottawa to lay the cornerstone of the Parliament Buildings' new Peace Tower, constructed to commemorate the over sixty thousand Canadians who gave their lives during the First World War. From Eastern Canada, the prince continued to Western Canada to visit the Prairie provinces and went as far as Vancouver and Victoria, in British Columbia. Affable and informal, Edward mixed easily among the crowds and played, to the delight of all, the role of Indian chief, cowpuncher, and baseball pitcher. On the last day of the trip, to the great astonishment of the crowd, he drove his own locomotive and, wearing his conductor's hat, waved out the locomotive's window to those assembled below.

In 1927, Edward returned to Canada with his younger brother George, later Duke of Kent, for another rail tour that took them across the country. This time, however, Canadian Pacific was obliged to share the honour of hosting the princes with its new arch-competitor, Canadian National Railway. It was perhaps fitting that during their visit, Edward inaugurated Toronto's new Union Station (the third station on the site), which would serve both lines.

Clockwise from top left:

King George VI and Queen Elizabeth on the outer deck of Canadian Pacific's *Empress of Australia*, May 6, 1939

Canadian Pacific's *Empress of Australia* leaving Portsmouth with the royal couple aboard, May 6, 1939

Elements of the British Home Fleet escorting the *Empress of Australia* off the Isle of Wight. Viewed from the stern of the *Empress of Australia*, May 6, 1939.

Two days late, on May 17, the *Empress of Australia* and the royal couple arrive at Quebec, with spectators watching from the Dufferin Terrace, in front of the Chateau Frontenac

1939: A REIGNING MONARCH SETS FOOT ON CANADIAN SOIL

In the spring of 1939, Canadian Pacific again played an instrumental role in the organization of a royal tour, with the triumphant visit of His Majesty King George VI and Her Majesty Queen Elizabeth. It was the first visit of a reigning monarch to Canada. Although Canadian National Railway shared some of the honour, Canadian Pacific's ships, hotels, and trains carried out the brunt of the work and enjoyed most of the visibility during the twenty-nine days and 13,800 kilometres (8,600 miles) of the royal itinerary.

The significance of this visit, not only for Canada but also the United Kingdom, must be emphasized. By the spring of 1939, it was obvious that war with Nazi Germany was looming, and the trip to Canada offered an opportunity to strengthen the emotional ties between the two countries. Ultimately, the royal visit served once again to help prepare the dominion for the sacrifices of the oncoming struggle. The King and Queen were a handsome and popular couple, but behind the royal presence was a very shy and retiring man with a strong stutter who had only reluctantly ascended to the throne after the stunning abdication in 1936 of his brother, Edward VIII.

The King refused the use of a major British warship to carry him to Canada because of the tense international situation. Instead, Canadian Pacific's *Empress of Australia* was given the unusual honour of flying the royal pennant and transporting the King and Queen. Tens of thousands of cheering citizens bade farewell to the royal couple at their departure from Southampton, with numerous warships of the Royal Navy escorting the *Empress of Australia*. The trip

Left: The royal couple's day in Quebec City ended with a banquet in the ballroom of the Chateau Frontenac. The following morning, they left the city on board a Canadian Pacific train, headed for Three Rivers and Montreal and then continued on to Ottawa.

Right: King George VI and Queen Elizabeth meeting First Nations chiefs at Calgary, May 26, 1939

was a major event for the world's press. The elegance of the *Empress of Australia* and the crew of over four hundred who served the royal party impressed the King and Queen. Heavy pack ice encountered in the approaches to Canada, however, caused a two-day delay.

After a week in Eastern Canada, the royal couple headed west for visits along the CPR line in Manitoba, Saskatchewan, and Alberta. On May 27, they had a day of rest at the Banff Springs Hotel. After their visit to British Columbia, the couple returned to Eastern Canada and embarked on a four-day trip to the eastern United States.

CP'S ROYAL TRADITION CONTINUES

Canadian Pacific has hosted many other members of the royal family, including Queen Elizabeth II and Prince Philip, who have been guests on a number of occasions at several Canadian Pacific hotels. Numerous non-British royalty have also been guests.

Perhaps the most remarkable was Princess Grace of Monaco, who served as Queen of the Quebec Winter Carnival during her stay at the Chateau Frontenac in February 1969. Of all the dignitaries and celebrities who visited the Chateau over the years, Grace Kelly most impressed the hotel staff. Those who served her stated that she was truly a beautiful person, "both inside and out."

Left: Queen Elizabeth and King George VI departing Vancouver May 31, 1939

Right: Queen Elizabeth II and Prince Philip entering the Chateau Frontenac, 1959

Overleaf: Sailors approaching the burning hulk of the *Empress of Britain*, October 26, 1940

WAR AND PEACE

Even before the launching of the second *Empress of Britain* in 1930, the world of travel had been turned on its head. The arrival of the automobile in the early twentieth century revolutionized travel patterns and diminished rail traffic. Initially, the change affected only short-distance travel plans, but with the construction of major western highways in the early 1920s, even longer vacations began to change. A new Great Circle Route was completed in 1923, with highways linking San Francisco via Salt Lake City to Yellowstone and Glacier National Parks, which in turn were linked by roads through the western Canadian mountains. American and Canadian vacationers could now visit the Canadian Rockies in their cars and return home without having used Canadian Pacific's railway system or its hotels. Nevertheless, the affluence of the 1920s meant the Canadian Pacific system remained highly successful, and the company was able to undertake major expansions of its hotels and shipping fleets. But the system was under stress, and the arrival of the Depression in 1929, followed by World War II, brought to an end the glory years the company had known for over three decades.

It is interesting to note that although the Great Depression badly hurt the company's overall profitability, upscale tourist traffic was less affected. As always in a deflationary period, those who had assets or fixed income saw the value of their money double and triple.

Canadian Pacific quickly reacted to the challenges of the new motor tourism. People travelling by car often wanted cheaper and quicker accommodations, the ability to travel by car now being the focus of the trip, rather than a stay in a single hotel. In 1923, Canadian Pacific opened the first of its bungalow camps to serve this new clientele and established a number of camps along the new roads in the mountains.

At the same time, the Brewster tour and transportation company, founded in 1892 to provide guide and backpacking services for guests at the Banff Springs Hotel, started to organize motorized touring in the mountains. By the early 1920s the company was offering guests "Motor Detours" in deluxe touring vehicles. The Fred Harvey Company's famous Indian Detour Tours, offered to travellers on the Santa Fe Railway in the American Southwest, probably inspired this endeavour.

WORLD WAR II

After the tremendous challenges of the Great Depression came the cataclysm of World War II. As it had during the First World War, Canadian Pacific placed all its vast resources at the disposal of the Allies. Its fleets transported over a million troops and civilians during the war and carried another million tons of cargo. A total of twelve of its vessels were lost directly to enemy action, the highest losses sustained by any of the Allied shipping companies during the conflict. At home, Canadian Pacific's trains transported hundreds of thousands of troops, and its factories produced crucial war materials. The company's efforts during both world wars were among its greatest legacies.

The loss of vessels to enemy action included the *Empress of Britain*. Caught by a long-range German bomber off the northwest Irish coast on the morning of October 26, 1940, she burned through the night. The next day, as she was being towed into Derry, Ireland, a German U-32 submarine fired two torpedoes at her, and she sank in the early morning hours of October 28. The *Empress* was the largest Allied liner lost to enemy action in World War II, and the largest vessel ever sunk by a U-boat. Her tonnage was almost a quarter larger than that of Cunard's *Lusitania*, sunk by a German submarine in the First World War.

————

Below: The Quebec Conferences of 1943 and 1944. From left to right: the Governor General of Canada, Major General The Earl of Athlone; the President of the United States, Franklin Delano Roosevelt; the Prime Minister of Great Britain, Sir Winston Churchill; the Prime Minister of Canada, William Lyon Mackenzie King.

Facing page left: Sir Winston Churchill and Prime Minister W.L.M. King with Canadian cabinet ministers at the entrance to the Chateau Frontenac during the Octagon Conference, September 14, 1944.

Facing page right: Eleanor Roosevelt on the arm of Prime Minister King, with Clementine Churchill behind them, ascending the staircase leading to the ballroom of the Chateau Frontenac, at the prime minister's reception held during the Octagon Conference of 1944.

Overleaf: Motor Detours, Canadian Pacific poster, c. 1920s

Overleaf, facing page: Couple in car at Banff, overlooking Lake Minnewanka and Sulphur Mountain, c. 1925

The company made great sacrifices, but it also enjoyed great triumphs. Canadian Pacific's Chateau Frontenac was chosen as the site of the August 1943 Quadrant Conference and the September 1944 Octagon Conference, led by President Roosevelt and Prime Minister Churchill to plan Allied strategy against the Axis forces. Over five hundred Allied staff officers came to the Chateau Frontenac to work on the high-level planning.

The participants at the Quadrant Conference made the decision to invade mainland Italy and approved the outline of the plan for the future invasion of Normandy. The Octagon Conference focused on finishing the war with the Japanese. With spitfire aircraft in the air and great anti-aircraft guns placed in front of the Chateau Frontenac on the Dufferin Terrace, the whole world was watching. It was a major moment for both Canada and Canadian Pacific.

THE POST–SECOND WORLD WAR PERIOD

After the Second World War, changes in travel patterns accelerated again, this time as a result of the increase in air travel. By 1958, Canadian Pacific flew more people to Europe than it carried by ship. In 1971, the last of its passenger liners had been permanently laid up, and in 1978 the company gave up all its passenger trains. "The World's Greatest Transportation System" had basically ceased to exist.

CANADIAN PACIFIC AIRLINES

Canadian Pacific Airlines was founded in 1942 with the amalgamation of ten different companies involved in regional air travel, mostly in the Canadian north. After intensive participation in the Canadian war effort of World War II, the company expanded its operations across Canada and overseas. Operating out of its home base in Vancouver, British Columbia, CPA specialized in flying a great circle, or polar, route to the Far East. The company ultimately reached five different continents, provided regular service across Canada, and operated numerous charter flights. Regular destinations included Hong Kong, Australia, New Zealand, South America, Israel, and Amsterdam. In 1986, the company became the first airline to operate non-stop flights from North America to China. A year later CPA was sold to Pacific Western Airlines, which later merged with Air Canada.

————

Left: CPA Boeing 747

Right: Passengers embarking a CPA DC3 in Vancouver, British Columbia, 1947

Facing page: CP aircraft, Canadian Pacific poster, 1956

CANADIAN PACIFIC'S LEGACY

The importance of Canadian Pacific's legacy to Canada is overwhelming. Its role in the development of the Canadian West was crucial for the creation of the country we know today. Its early promotional efforts helped Canada to earn world recognition and created a positive image of the young nation that still resonates around the globe. As for the country's citizens, Canadian Pacific's story is one of the key elements that define the Canadian identity and help unite this enormous and very diverse nation.

Across the country, Canadian Pacific's legacy is still visible to Canadians. The freight operations of Canadian Pacific, one of North America's largest railways, remain a crucial element of the Canadian economy. And the distinctive architecture of the great railway hotels and stations, inspired by Canadian Pacific's aristocratic style, still dominates the central cores and skylines of Canada's major cities.

CP'S RAILWAY STATIONS

Many of the hundreds of railway stations that Canadian Pacific built along its different lines are gone today, but in their time they played a crucial role in the communities they served. Not only did they serve as a physical and emotional link to the outside world, but often they were also gathering points for the community.

Most of the stations were simple rectangular structures with gable roofs and bay windows that created a picturesque style. The size of the building depended on the importance of the stop. Some of the larger ones had two storeys, with the station master living above the station. Restaurants, gardens, and hotels were often located nearby. But in major centres, the company hired important architects to construct impressive structures in the leading international styles of the day: Romanesque, Beaux Arts, or Canadian Pacific's dearly beloved Chateau style.

Below: McAdam Station, New Brunswick

Preceding pages: The Banff Springs Hotel in winter

McAdam, New Brunswick, Station

In 1889, Canadian Pacific constructed the Short Line across the State of Maine to link Montreal to its winter port of Saint John, New Brunswick, the St. Lawrence River being frozen over during the winter months. Located on the border between New Brunswick and Maine, McAdam served as an important rail junction between the Short Line and an American line running to the south and was the point of customs where travellers would enter into Canada.

Because upper-class Canadian and American travellers summering at nearby Saint Andrews would use the station, William Van Horne, the president of the line, likely oversaw the design and construction of the enormous McAdam Station. These travellers included Van Horne and many of the Canadian Pacific elite who had summer homes at Saint Andrews; some, like Van Horne, travelling by private rail car. Completed in 1901 by the Montreal architect Edward Maxwell and enlarged in 1910–11 by W.S. Painter, the long, rectangular, two-and-a-half-storey stone structure was unusual in that it served as a combined station and hotel,

with seventeen guest rooms located on the second floor, and rooms for female staff on the third. Downstairs were the offices and waiting room, as well as dining room facilities that could handle as many as two thousand passengers a day. The steeply pitched roofs, tower, and dormer windows make the structure one of the best examples of a station constructed in the company's Chateau style, and the edifice incorporates the finest building materials with many highly ornate architectural details.

Via Rail passenger service ended at the McAdam Station in 1994 when Canadian Pacific gave up its line, and the building, designated a National Historic Site in 1976, now serves as a museum.

Above: Gare du Palais, Quebec City

Gare du Palais Station, Quebec City

Opened in 1916, in Quebec City's Lower Town, the Gare du Palais (Palace Station) was constructed by Canadian Pacific in the same Chateau style as the company's nearby railway hotel, the Chateau Frontenac. The station's steep copper roofs, pointed towers, and multiple dormer windows convey to those arriving in the city by train a strong sense of the romance and French traditions of historic Quebec.

However, the great glory of the building is its enormous entrance hall, with warm brick walls and marble floors crowned by a massive vaulted and glazed ceiling. The station are colourfully decorated with numerous mosaics and stained-glass images representing the city's romantic past, the development of Canada, and the prowess of Canadian Pacific. The building is a masterpiece.

From 1976 to 1985, the Gare du Palais was no longer in service as a train station. After a major restoration, it reopened to serve as an intermodal transportation hub for the city. Its restoration has played a major role in the revitalization of Quebec's Lower Town and continues to offer the traveller a wonderful entrance point to the city.

Waterfront Station, Vancouver

Canadian Pacific Railway opened Vancouver's present-day Waterfront Station in August 1914. Built by a Montreal architectural firm in the neo-classical style, the structure marked a dramatic change from the company's previous station, which had been built in the typical Chateau style. The station served as Canadian Pacific's western terminus until 1979. Today, the structure is a major public terminal for a number of different transportation modes.

More than a dozen Ionic columns adorn the exterior of the building, and the interior walls are painted with murals that depict the scenery one would view during a transcontinental train ride with Canadian Pacific. The wife of a CPR executive painted these murals.

Clockwise from left:

Vancouver's Waterfront Station

The entrance hall of the Gare du Palais

The interior of Vancouver's Waterfront Station

THE HOTELS

The most obvious aspect of the Canadian Pacific legacy is Canada's great railway hotels, many of which were built by Canadian Pacific or were influenced in their construction by the company's Chateau style. Canadian Pacific operated two types of railway hotels: urban hotels located near the company's rail stations that served both professional and leisure travellers, and rural resort hotels situated in locations with majestic scenery that made them travel destinations in themselves.

To reinforce its position, in 1988 Canadian Pacific bought up the hotels and resorts of its great competitor, Canadian National Railway, bringing its ownership of historic Canadian hotel properties to over sixteen. At the turn of the twenty-first century, the company continued this commitment to its railway heritage by investing over a billion dollars to restore, and in some cases enlarge, many of its landmark properties.

For investment purposes, Canadian Pacific in 2001 separated its five subsidiaries — rail, ships (cargo), petroleum, coal, and hotels — into discrete entities. One of the newly formed companies, Canadian Pacific Hotels, had already joined forces with the Fairmont Hotel chain in the United States to create a leading luxury hotel management company, Fairmont Hotels and Resorts. With its headquarters in Toronto, Fairmont manages properties that include almost all of Canadian Pacific's historic hotels. The hotels themselves were sold to separate owners.

With properties located around the globe, Fairmont today is one of the world's largest hotel management companies. Its hotels include some of the most famous icons of the Golden Age of Travel: the Savoy in London, the Plaza in New York, and Fairmont Peace Hotel in Shanghai. It may not have the trains and ships that Canadian Pacific once had, but Fairmont's global scope is worthy of its extraordinary beginnings as the Canadian company which at one time "spanned the world."

Fairmont Chateau Lake Louise

Magnificently located on the shores of Lake Louise, below the Victoria Glacier, Chateau Lake Louise is one of Canada's best-known resort hotels and landmarks. Initially constructed by Canadian Pacific in 1890 as a log cabin for outdoor adventurers and alpinists, the chateau was continually expanded in the years leading up to World War I.

After a major fire, a large concrete hotel was completed on the site in 1925, and it remained intact until the 1980s, when another major expansion occurred. In recent years, the hotel has undergone major upgrades, making it into a luxury alpine resort. In 2004, the new Mount Temple

Below and facing page: Fairmont Chateau Lake Louise

Wing opened. Today, the Fairmont Chateau Lake Louise has over 550 rooms and offers its guests numerous outdoor activities and programs. Winter sports are a major component of the hotel's activities. Since the Calgary Winter Olympics in 1988, skiing has become a major attraction for the area, with the nearby Lake Louise Ski Resort hosting each November the first of the World Cup ski races.

Fairmont Banff Springs Hotel

The first of Canadian Pacific's resort hotels, the Banff Springs opened its doors in 1888. Overlooking the Bow River Valley and Mount Rundle, with the Fairholme Range in the distance, the hotel offered its visitors one of the finest mountain views in all of North America.

The castle-like Banff Springs proved very popular and soon became a destination in its own right. The building underwent continuous expansion from 1900 through to 1928. But the property struggled to maintain its success in the post-World War II period, until promotional efforts to target foreign markets and the opening of the hotel in the winter months for skiers revived its clientele. The 1980s and 90s saw another period of major expansion for the resort with the Fairmont Banff Springs growing to 770 rooms, and the construction of a major conference centre and the luxury spa, Solace.

Today this aristocratic structure and its extraordinary location offer a dream-like destination for anyone seeking a romantic visit. Along with the Chateau Frontenac, the iconic Banff Springs is one of the country's best-known and most beloved structures. It is the epitome of the dream that Van Horne had for the promotion of Canadian Pacific and the newly established country of Canada.

Clockwise from below:

Mount Stephen Hall, Fairmont Banff Springs Hotel, named for Lord Mount Stephen, the founder of the Canadian Pacific Railway

Fairmont Banff Springs Hotel, Riverview Lounge

Fairmont Banff Springs Hotel

Fairmont Hotel Vancouver

The Hotel Vancouver is the third Canadian Pacific Hotel of this name in Vancouver. The first was a plain five-storey structure that opened in 1888, and the second a much more grandiose structure in the Italian Renaissance style that opened in 1916. With its wonderful rooftop tea garden, the second hotel remained a centre of Vancouver social life until just before World War II.

The present Hotel Vancouver took eleven years to build and opened in 1939, in time for the royal tour of King George VI and Queen Elizabeth. Boasting majestic public rooms, the Fairmont Hotel Vancouver is truly an elegant and regal structure. A major restoration in the mid-1990s has ensured that this breathtaking and historic building remains at the forefront of Vancouver's best hotels.

Right: The lobby of the Fairmont Hotel Vancouver

Far right: The ballroom of the Fairmont Hotel Vancouver

Fairmont Royal York

When Canadian Pacific opened the twenty-eight-storey Royal York Hotel in 1929, it was the tallest building in the city — and the whole of the British Empire. A state-of-the-art hotel for the time, it offered a radio and a private shower or bath in each of its 1,048 rooms. It opened on the eve of the Great Depression, and Canadian Pacific's chairman, Sir Edward Beatty, was strongly criticized over its construction, but the hotel proved profitable right from the start. With its prime location across the street from Toronto's Union Station and the magnificence of its lobby and public rooms, the Royal York since its inception has played a prominent role in Toronto's public life. It has also been the residence of choice for Queen Elizabeth and other members of the royal family when they stay in Toronto. The Queen usually has an entire floor of the hotel, with a special royal suite, reserved for her and her party.

Left: The lobby of the Fairmont Royal York, Toronto

Far left: The ballroom of the Fairmont Royal York, Toronto

Overleaf: Fairmont Royal York, Toronto

Overleaf, facing page: Fairmont Hotel Vancouver, nighttime view

Fairmont Empress Hotel

Designed by local architect Francis Rattenbury as a terminus hotel for Canadian Pacific's steamship line, the Empress Hotel is the centrepiece of the magnificent Inner Harbour of beautiful Victoria, British Columbia, the province's capital.

The hotel opened in 1908, and additional wings were added between 1909 and 1914 and in 1928. The Empress has often hosted royalty, including the dashing Prince of Wales in 1919, and King George VI and Queen Elizabeth during their tour of Canada in 1939.

Today, the Fairmont Empress has 477 rooms, most of which overlook the Inner Harbour or the hotel's beautiful gardens. The interior decoration and public rooms are exquisite and offer a sense of Edwardian romance and the grandeur of the British Empire. Of special note is the hotel's Bengal Lounge, which is decorated in a colonial East Indian style. Rudyard Kipling, a guest of the hotel, would certainly have felt at home there.

Top: The Empress Room restaurant, Fairmont Empress Hotel, Victoria, BC

Middle: The Empress Room restaurant, Fairmont Empress Hotel, Victoria, BC

Bottom: The Bengal Room, Fairmont Empress Hotel, Victoria, BC

Facing page: Fairmont Empress Hotel, Victoria, British Columbia

Fairmont Chateau Laurier

Magnificently located at the entrance of the Rideau Canal to the Ottawa River, the Fairmont Chateau Laurier is one of country's most elegant and picturesque railway hotels. It was opened in 1912 by a major competitor of Canadian Pacific, the Grand Trunk Railway. The company's president, Charles Melville Hays, decided to emulate his adversaries and built the Chateau Laurier in Canadian Pacific's Chateau style. The Grand Trunk used the same style for its Fort Garry Hotel, opened in Winnipeg in 1913, and the Hotel Macdonald, opened in Edmonton in 1915.

The finest building materials were used in the construction of the Chateau Laurier, including Italian marble and Indiana limestone. Canadian Pacific took over the Chateau Laurier in 1988.

———

Right: Zoe's Lounge, Fairmont Chateau Laurier, Ottawa

Far right: Fairmont Chateau Laurier, Ottawa, with the locks of the Rideau Canal in the foreground

Below: Fairmont Chateau Laurier ballroom

Below right: Fairmont Chateau Laurier Hotel, Ottawa, Ontario

Fairmont Chateau Frontenac

The Chateau Frontenac is one of the best-known public buildings in Canada and all of North America. Its majestic silhouette of towers and turrets with steep copper roofs, rises above the old walled City of Quebec and, from its clifftop perch, dominates the city skyline and the mighty St. Lawrence River below.

Initially constructed on the site of the residence of the Governor of New France, the Chateau was named for Louis de Buade, comte de Frontenac, a long-time governor of the colony. The Chateau served Canadian Pacific as an Atlantic terminus for its trains and ships and eventually became a destination in itself. Such was the building's mystique that, in the early days, it was marketed in Europe as the "Gateway to the New Route to the Orient."

The hotel remains as popular as ever and is an icon of Canada and Old Quebec. A new wing was added to the building for its centenary year in 1993, and in 2015 a major restoration and renovation was completed to enhance the Chateau's historic prestige and glamour.

Clockwise from above:

The ballroom of the Fairmont Chateau Frontenac

The Verchères Room of the Fairmont Chateau Frontenac

The great chandelier above the staircase leading to the Rose Room

The lobby of the Chateau Frontenac

The Algonquin Hotel

A four-storied, half-timbered building, the Algonquin Hotel was opened in 1889 by an American businessman hoping to attract investors to Saint Andrews, a beautiful town located on a peninsula on New Brunswick's Passamaquoddy Bay, a body of water linked to the high tides of the Bay of Fundy. In 1903, Canadian Pacific purchased the hilltop property and built a fine golf course to attract summer visitors travelling to the town via the company's new Short Line Railway across Maine. The resort became very popular, especially for the CPR elite, including William Van Horne, who built elegant summer homes and gardens nearby.

A fire ravaged the Algonquin in 1914, and the company rebuilt the structure in concrete, with a charming Tudor-style facade that the building still retains. Numerous heads of state and royalty have stayed at the hotel, including presidents of the United States Theodore Roosevelt, Franklin Delano Roosevelt, and Lyndon B. Johnson, and Charles, Prince of Wales, with Princess Diana. In 1970, Canadian Pacific sold the hotel to local interests, but it was continuously operated, first by Canadian Pacific Hotels and then by Fairmont Hotels, until 2011.

And so Canadian Pacific's story comes full circle, with the expansion of Fairmont Hotels around the world and into the Orient. The vision of George Stephen and William Van Horne had always been grand. They had seen the potential of a young country and used its strategic advantages to create a transportation system without parallel in world history. In doing so, they helped to unite this vast and diverse country, to build the West, and to project a positive image of Canada around the world. Today, Canadian Pacific no longer offers a passenger service, but you can still enjoy the spectacular scenery along the tracks that the company built, travelling across Canada by train with VIA Rail, and in the West with Rocky Mountaineer. As Canada moves forward, one can only hope that the company's legacy and achievements will help inspire future generations of Canadians to follow in Canadian Pacific's footsteps and take on the world.

———

Below: The Algonquin Hotel

Facing page: The Chateau Frontenac and Dufferin Terrace viewed during the winter months

Overleaf: Canadian Pacific poster of Chateau Lake Louise, c. 1938

Overleaf, facing page: The Canadian Pacific household flag designed by Sir William Van Horne. A "straight flush" indeed.

Further Reading

For general works about Canadian Pacific I would like to suggest W. Kaye Lamb's *History of the Canadian Pacific Railway* (Toronto: MacMillan, 1977), David Cruise's *Lords of the Line: The Men Who Built the CPR* (Toronto: Penguin, 1989), and John A. Eagle's *The Canadian Pacific Railway and the Development of Western Canada, 1896–1914* (Montreal: McGill-Queens University Press, 1989).

Graeme Pole's *Gravity, Steam and Steel: An Illustrated Railway History of Rogers Pass* (Markham, Ontario: Fifth House Publishing, 2012) and *The Spiral Tunnels and the Big Hill: A Canadian Adventure* (Calgary: Altitude Publishing, 1995) give a sense of the dramatic nature of the construction of the line.

Gordon Turner's *Empress of Britain: Canadian Pacific's Greatest Ship* (Calgary: Altitude Publishing, 1995) and Robert D. Turner's *The Pacific Empresses* (Winlaw, BC: Sono Nis Press, 1981) deal with elements of Canadian Pacific's maritime history.

For tourism there is E.J. Hart's *The Selling of Canada: The CPR and the Beginnings of Canadian Tourism* (Calgary: Altitude Publishing, 1983) and the works of the CP archivist David Laurence Jones, *Famous Name Trains: Travelling in Style with the CPR* (Markham, Ontario: Fifth House Publishing, 2006) and *See This World Before the Next: Cruising with CPR Steamships in the Twenties and Thirties* (Markham, Ontario: Fifth House Publishing, 2004).

On the hotels look for Barbara Chisholm, ed., *Castles of the North: Canada's Grand Hotels* (Toronto: LYNX, 2001) and France Gagnon Prattes's *The Château Frontenac* and *The Banff Springs Hotel: The Castle in the Rockies* (Quebec: Éditions Continuité, 1999 and 2001).

For first-person accounts of early travel with CP, Edward Roper's *By Track and Trail* (London: W.H. Allen, 1891) and M.F. Bridie's *Round the World Without a Pinprick: Being the Diary Of M.F. Bridie, Passenger on the First World Cruise of the RMS Empress of Britain, 1931–1932* (Birmingham, UK: Jones & Co., 1932) are the best accounts available.

Finally, for the wonderful art work of Canadian Pacific look for Marc H. Choko and David L. Jones's *Posters of the Canadian Pacific* (Toronto: Firefly Publishing, 2004).

Preceding pages: Canadian Pacific brochure, 1913.

Illustration Credits

Courtesy of the Algonquin Resorts: 193 (Photographer Gary Kan)

Courtesy of Andrew Nugara: 19

Author's Collection: front cover (background image and figures), back flap, 4-5, 6, 9, 18, 22 top, 25 top, 28, 35 top, 58-59, 60 top, 60 middle, 60 bottom, 72-73, 74, 85 top, 85 bottom, 89 top, 89 bottom, 106-107 bottom, 110, 110-111 bottom, 114 bottom left, 120 top, 121 top, 143 top, 143 bottom, 146, 150, 151, 156 top left, 156 left and right, 164-165, 170 left, 195, 200

By permission of the Canadian Pacific Archives, Montreal: back cover (6044), 10-11 (NS 1960), 19 top (M.1266), 23 (BR311), 39 (A6343), 43 (A12345), 44 (A12358), 47 top (NS12968), 52-53 (A17333), 56 (BR 124-2), 57 (BR 124-1), 75 (A20297), 80 (A6352), 88 (NC-53-52), 96 (BR.179), 97 (A17295-R), 99 (A635), 105 (A6358), 107 top right (NS10949), 108 (A28394), 109 (NS15170), 112 bottom (M707), 113 bottom (25806) 114 (bottom right) (A6131), 115 (M794), 120 bottom (A6024), 122-123 (NS12276), 124 top (A6694), 124 bottom (A6058), 125 (NS12258), 126-127 (A6037), 130 (BR290), 131 (A6326), 132-33 centre (A26312), 133 right (A37318), 142 (6044), 144-145 (A10152), 170 (A20693), 194 (A6124)

Courtesy of the City of Vancouver Archives: 29 (AM 54-S4-BO P154), 116 (99-2715), 117 top (99-2716), 118 top (99-5050), 118 (bottom right) (AM-S4-Port-P250), 155 (AM54-S4 Duke C & Y P16.3, Mathews Collection) 156 bottom left (AM54-SGN 377, Mathews Collection), 156 bottom right (AM54-Duke C & Y P12, Mathews Collection), 159 top (AM54-S4 Duke C & Y P16.1) 159 middle (AM1535-CVA99827), 159 bottom (AM54-S4-Port-N840.2) 163 left (6-244)

Courtesy of Fairmont Hotels & Resorts: 121 bottom, 172-173, 178, 179, 180 all, 181, 182 all, 183 all, 184, 185, 186, 187 all, 188 all, 189 all, 190, 191 top left, 191 top right, 192

Courtesy of Gino Gariepy. (Jack Hayward Photographer): 112 top left, 112 top right, 113 top left, 113 top right

By permission of the Glenbow Archives, Calgary: 14 (NA-674-36), 25 bottom (NA-3740-29), 46-47 bottom (NA-984-2), 54 top (GL PAM 971), 54 bottom (GA NA-1284-1), 55 (Private Collection), 65 top (NA-387-21), 68 top (NA-4967-10), 69 top (NA-1075-12), 91 (NA-719-7), 154 (NA-140-1)

Courtesy of Gordon Price, wwwpricetags.word.press.com: 176-177 bottom, 177 top

Courtesy of Ian Boyle of Simplon Postcards, UK: 34-35 bottom

By permission of the Library of Congress 84 (LC-USZC4-2353-CALL NO. POS-CAN.C3 NO. 2

By permission of Luc-Antoine Couturier: 175, 176 top left, 191 bottom

By permission of the Manitoba Provincial Archives: 36-37 (N4719)

Courtesy of the McAdam Historical Restoration Commission: 174 (Gail Swan photographer)

By permission of the McCord Museum, Montreal: 15 top (I-63346), 15 bottom (II-81628), 16 (MP.1993.7.15), 17 (MP-0000.158.29), 22 bottom (MP-1993.6.1.22), 24 (View 2135), 26-27 (View-2945), 65 bottom (View-3115.3), 157 top (View-6799), 157 bottom (View-6831)

Courtesy of McGill University: 76 bottom (Maxwell Archives, Blackader-Lauterman Library), 104 (RBSC), 173 (RBSC)

By permission of the National Portrait Gallery, London: 80 (NPG 1863)

By permission of the Peabody Essex Museum, Salem, Massachusetts, and the Phillips Library Collection: 83 (Bradlee Collection, Life on Shipboard no. 13. Negative 13736, Accession number: PH235)

By permission of the Provincial Archives of Alberta: 2-3 (PR1967.0143.203), 13 (P101), 106 top left (W. Hanson Borne: B9785)

By permission of the Public Archives of Canada: front cover, map detail (ANC 137959), 12 (C002774), 20-21 (PA_066576), 42 (PA-173009), 45 (C-009660), 46 bottom right (PA-010264), 50-51 (PA-029966), 62-63 (PA-031944), 66 bottom right (PA-026285), 68 bottom (PA-122676), 78 (PA-024760), 82 (PA-0211374), 103 (PA-3192785), 158 (PA-11848), 166 left (NFB-1964-087, C-071095), 166 right (NFB-1964-087, Box 1215, C-026934), 167 (NFB-1964-087-C-021525 C-026921), 171 (PA-804144)

By permission of the Quebec Provincial Archives: 76 top (P547,S1,SS1,SSS1,D1-14), 77 (03Q_P547,S1,SS1,SSS1,D001P3494), 79 (P547,S1,SS1,SSS1,D1-14), 100-101 (P428,S3,SS1,D13,P-14-39), 111 bottom (P560,S2,D2,P117652-1), 161 bottom (P428,S3,SS1, D7,P33) 162 left (P600,S6,D1,P578), 163 right (P600,S6,D1,P695)

By permission of the Quebec City Archives: 111 top (17113), 111 centre (17297)

By permission of the Royal BC Museum, BC Archives: 19 middle (A-08713)

Courtesy of Steven Given, Australia: 138-139

By permission of the Smithsonian Institution Archives: 98 bottom (Record Unit 95 Box 23 Folder 23, 2002-10626)

By permission of the Toronto City Archives: 152-53 (Fonds 1266, Item 11128)

Courtesy of the Toronto Reference Library: 170 right

By permission of the University of Alberta, Peel Collection: 48-49 (PC-004504), 51 top right (PC-001267)

By permission of the University of British Columbia, Chung Collection: 30-31 top centre (PH-0261), 31 top right (PH-02426), 38 top (EX-WW3) 38 bottom (4045), 40-41 (GR-00072), 61 top right (PH-02901), 61 bottom (CC-249-5 Box 249), 66 bottom left (PH-0209), 119 (PH-06859), 128-129 (PH-02953), 132 left (PH-03697), 135 (PH-04952), 136 top (PH-04943), 136 bottom (PH-04963), 137 top (PH-04952), 137 centre (PH-04962), 137 bottom (PH-04679), 140-141 (Box 221, album Empress of Britain II World Cruise 1931-32), 147 (PH-02511), 148 (PH-02765), 149 (PH-02859), 160 top left (PH-05195), 160-161 top centre (PH-03707), 161 top right (PH-05198), 162 right (PH-05207), 196-197 (box 249-album 4)

By permission of the Vancouver Maritime Museum: 31 (2004.0095.0001), 117 bottom (19566)

By permission of the Vancouver Public Library: 30 left (12866), 118 bottom left (23361)

By permission of the Victoria and Albert Museum, London: 32-33 (PP.8.D-E)

By permission of the Whyte Museum of the Canadian Rockies: 61 top left (V653/NA-30), 64 (V653/NG-255), 67 bottom (NA66-1594), 69 bottom (V653-NA-021), 70-71 (V653-NA-20), 86-87 (V527-PS-2-31), 90 (V527-PS-1-264), 92 (V653-NA-783), 93 (V653-NA-181), 94 top left (V439-PS-6), 94 bottom right (V653-PS-130), 94-95 top (V527-PS-3-21), 95 bottom right (V527-PS-1-343), 98 top (V527-PS-1-274), 106-107 top centre (V263/NA-4838)

Copyright © 2015 by Éditions Sylvain Harvey.

All rights reserved. No part of this work may be reproduced or used in any form or by any means, electronic or mechanical, including photocopying, recording, or any retrieval system, without the prior written permission of the publisher or a licence from the Canadian Copyright Licensing Agency (Access Copyright). To contact Access Copyright, visit www.accesscopyright.ca or call 1-800-893-5777.

Simultaneously published in French by Éditions Sylvain Harvey under the title Canadien pacifique : L'empire du voyage (ISBN: 978-2-923794-73-0).

Edited by John Sweet.
Art direction and graphic design by André Durocher (Syclone).
Cover design by Julie Scriver.
Front cover illustrations: passenger train entering eastern portal of the Connaught tunnel, c. 1920; figures detailed from "Resorts in the Rockies," Canadian Pacific brochure cover, 1931, artist E.A. Odell; map detailed from a Canadian Pacific Poster, 1895.
Back cover illustration: The Empress of Britain poster.
Back flap illustration: Early Canadian Pacific travel poster/postcard.

Printed in Canada.
10 9 8 7 6 5 4 3 2 1

Library and Archives Canada Cataloguing in Publication

Lane, Barry, 1952-, author
    Canadian Pacific : the golden age of travel / Barry Lane.

ISBN 978-0-86492-878-8 (bound)

1. Canadian Pacific Railway Company--History. 2. Canadian Pacific Railway Company--Pictorial works. 3. Railroads--Canada--History. 4. Railroads--Canada--Pictorial works. I. Title.

HE2810.C2L28 2015   385.0971   C2015-904093-0

We acknowledge the generous support of the Government of Canada, the Canada Council for the Arts, and the Government of New Brunswick.

Nous reconnaissons l'appui généreux du gouvernement du Canada, du Conseil des arts du Canada, et du gouvernement du Nouveau-Brunswick.

Goose Lane Editions
500 Beaverbrook Court, Suite 330
Fredericton, New Brunswick
CANADA E3B 5X4
www.gooselane.com

Overleaf: Canadian Pacific poster, The Empress of Scotland, formerly the Kaiserin Auguste Victoria, c. 1921-1930

CANADIAN PACIFIC
SPANS THE WORLD

MOST CONVENIENT ROUTE TO
CANADA – U.S.A. – JAPAN – CHINA, NEW ZEALAND & AUSTRALIA.